BOOKTALK

D0513189

AIDAN CHAMBERS

BOOKTALK

Occasional Writing on
Literature and
Children

THE BODLEY HEAD
LONDON

British Library Cataloguing
in Publication Data
Chambers, Aidan
Booktalk: occasional writing on literature
and children.
1. Children's literature—History and criticism
I. Title
809'.89282   PN1009.A1
ISBN 0-370-30858-1

© Aidan Chambers 1985
Printed in Great Britain for
The Bodley Head Ltd
9 Bow Street, London WC2E 7AL
by Redwood Burn Ltd, Trowbridge
First published 1985

CONTENTS

Preface

One evening after dark the five-year-old granddaughter of a friend of mine came to visit him. All alone she had walked from her house to his along a poorly lit path that led her through a forbidding parcel of trees. 'But weren't you afraid?' her grandfather asked. 'No, no, Grandpa,' she replied. 'All the way here I told myself the story of Little Red Riding Hood.'

This collection of occasional writing deals with story, children, and the adults who bring the two together. Common to all the pieces is a preoccupation with talk about books as a literary and an educational activity. All were written after 'The Reader in the Book', which was prepared in 1976 and first published in 1977. This marked a turning point in my critical and educational thinking, just as *Breaktime*, written during the same period, was a turning point in my fictional work.

Much of what follows was made for speaking to particular audiences, and as I could never be sure that everyone shared the ideas I regard as fundamental, there is inevitably some repetition and restatement. I have cleared away as much as I can, and hope for your patience with whatever overlapping remains. I have also done some minor editorial work on most of the previously published pieces.

The arrangement of the book follows a modest pattern. The first essay sets out commonplace wisdom about children and their reading. The next four concentrate on literature, how we think about it, and its relationship with children. Two articles about my own work follow, one of them a previously unpublished reading of *Breaktime* and *Dance on my Grave*. The final three pieces talk about teaching literature, whether to adults who teach children or to children themselves. The last of these is also the most recently written and appears here for the first time, a result of a continuing seminar with five teachers.

Two routine matters. First, the word 'text' now presents problems. Does it mean the text which is the work, the book itself, as in ordinary usage? Or does it mean the intangible *gestalt* held in language and experienced within us as we read and afterwards in our memories? The distinction matters in modern critical discussion, and it can't be ignored. I've used a capital, as Text, when I mean the intangible *gestalt*. Second, we surely must soon find a personal pronoun that includes male and female gender. I am so irritated by the domination of the masculine in English that I deliberately make the point here and there by using s/he and him/her.

Not in any way routine are the thanks I owe many people. All the teachers named in the following pages, especially those who allowed me to quote them. Hundreds of children who have talked to me with tolerance and generosity. Those organizers in many countries who trusted me with invitations to speak at meetings, at the risk of their reputations, and out of which these writings came. Those from whose books I quote. And these friends who have advised, sustained, and aided: Alan Tucker, Gordon Dennis, my editor Margaret Clark, and above all my wife, Nancy.

Aidan Chambers
South Woodchester
February 1985

The Role
of Literature
in Children's Lives

In 1981 the International Association of School Librarianship invited me to give the opening lecture in a section of their annual conference titled 'School Libraries for All?: The Special Child'. That year the tenth-anniversary gathering of the Association was held at the College of Librarianship at Aberystwyth, Wales. My task was to rehearse in a straightforward fashion, for an audience of school librarians from many countries, speaking many languages, the general ideas about literature and children that most of us share. The lecture is included here for the same reason; it's a place to begin, a summary of key thoughts that occur throughout the rest of this book.

*

A friend of mine is a tireless collector of funny stories. The other day he sent me one he'd heard on the radio at a time when I'm groaning at my desk. He tells me I work at the very times when the best funny stories can be heard on the radio. He's able to listen then for a reason that might interest you.

He was a teacher for some years and then quit because he could not come to terms with an extraordinary irony of British secondary school life. He taught English, and his passionate belief was and is that teaching literature is an occupation of the highest value. But he soon discovered, as I had before him, that the demands of our school system meant that all his time was spent on work that actually prevented him and his pupils from doing much reading of literature. He never had time, in school or out, to do more than gut the few set books he had to study with his students for various exams. Reading for himself, and with self-sought pleasure, was squashed into the tired corners of his life. He knew that a teacher of literature can only

I

teach well if he reads widely and deeply for himself, so in the end he quit. Now he does shift work in a factory and has all the time for reading that he wants—and gets better paid too.

As I say, my friend sent me a funny story told by a taxi-driver who picked up Bertrand Russell. The driver said, 'I knew it was Bertrand Russell straightaway. When he got sat down I turned round and said to him, "Now, Mr Russell, what's it all about then?" And do you know, he couldn't tell me!'

At this moment I tremble before you on the brink of that awful question, 'What's it all about then?' In case I fall over the edge and die the death screaming, 'I can't tell you!' I have divided what I want to say into two parts. I decided this when I realized my title implies two kinds of role. There is the role literature plays in children's inner lives—what literature does for them. And there is the role it can play in their exterior lives—the part literature should occupy in the environment where they live.

The first part is chilly with theories and assumptions we find it hard to demonstrate conclusively. They don't exactly require an act of faith to accept, but we still have a long way to go before we can prove everything we think we know. The second part is as practical and easy to sort out as the instructions for opening a can of beans. But anything practical only commands attention when one accepts the theory, the reason and worth of doing something. No one bothers with the instructions if they don't want the beans in the can.

The brochure for our meeting tells us that we shall be examining the needs of some special groups in the school community. But in one sense we are all special. We are all individuals with our own special needs, gifts, handicaps, peculiarities, hangups. Equally, whatever else may be true of the people we will be talking about—adults and children—we are the same in one fundamental and overridingly important way. We are all human beings. And the thing that's important about literature is this. It concerns itself with one of the few attributes that make us human: language. Not just language itself, for birds seem to have a kind of language, and dolphins, and, I can testify on personal experience, such little creatures as bees. So not just language, but language used in the particular form we call narrative, in which I include stories and poems and drama and the kind of writing that tries to tell us what happened, to whom, and why.

I would go as far as to say that it is this particular use of language—

the literary use that some have called 'storying'—that defines humanity and makes us human. I would say this particular form of language and our skill in using it empower us in being what we are, and make it possible for us to conceive of being more than we are. But this suggestion reaches towards that unwelcome act of faith I promised not to ask for, so leave aside such provocation for now.

Books have been written about the value of literature. There is no hope I can capture everything here in a paragraph or two. But some people have tried to boil it all down into a catchy sentence. None of them has succeeded, of course, but I do like one of these efforts. It's the one by Ezra Pound that goes: 'Literature is the news that stays news.' Pound was poking at that aspect of the role of literature that I want to concentrate on because it is especially pertinent to our theme today. Keeping in mind that literature is a unique relationship between language and form, let me join the ranks of those foolish enough to try to make a catch-all sentence:

Literature offers us images to think with.

Imagine what life is like for a newborn baby. All those crowding sensations of touch, taste, smell, hearing, sight. Chaos. An assault. Survival depends on making sense of all that data.

Living beyond survival to the point of being a culture-building species requires that we not only make sense of our surroundings, and of ourselves, but that we communicate our understandings, and, even more important, develop an ability to project ahead of ourselves, foreseeing causes and effects before they become active in our lives. Crudely speaking, this means we have to find a way of naming the data we receive, and then of putting them together in various patterns that help us see what can be done—and what are the consequences of what can be done—before we actually bring them into being. In short, we have to become not just manipulators but creators of ourselves and our environment.

How do we do this? As with all things human, the answer is as simple as it is complicated. The anthropologists report, my children's encyclopaedia says, that 'wherever there are men there is language', and wherever there are people they use language to tell stories.

Gossip is the most basic form of storytelling. Gossip is the story of our lives told by our tongues in daily episodes. Gossip can be like soap opera, entertaining but trivial. But sometimes gossip possesses a curiously powerful significance that reaches beyond one time and place, being handed down year after year from person to person, changed a little here, polished a little there. Then it becomes what we now call folk tale. When this kind of gossip is about God (or gods, if you want) it becomes myth. When it is about the strange, unnatural phenomena of life, it becomes fairy tale. Gossip in which we try to get to the essence of something, try to concentrate our experience rather than unpack it, tends to become poetry—what Auden, I think, called 'memorable speech'.

But however we classify that kind of talk, the important truth is that we all do it. In one way or another we all tell ourselves and each other stories about life. Adults may think about the world in other ways too, of course; but there is a significant thing about children and stories to which we must pay attention. James Moffett puts it like this in *Teaching the Universe of Discourse*:

> Whereas adults differentiate their thought with specialized kinds of discourse, generalization, and theory, children must, for a long time, make narrative do for all. They utter themselves almost entirely through stories—real or invented—and they apprehend what others say through story. The young learner, that is, does not talk and read explicitly about categories and theories of experience, he talks and reads about characters, events, and settings [which are] charged with symbolic meaning because they are tokens standing for unconscious classes and postulations of experience . . . [p. 49]

'Children must make narrative do for all.' If that is true, we hardly need make any other claim for the primary role literature plays in children's lives, whatever else may be their special individual needs. Nor would we require any other claim for the importance of libraries, though it also tells us something about the kind of libraries children need.

There's a little more I want to say yet before we get through with the chilly theory. (I like that word 'chilly' attached to theory because chilly can mean cold and miserable and rather unpleasant, which is what I find most people think when you mention the word theory. But chilli can also mean something mouth-scorchingly hot that gets the taste buds so excited they're almost hysterical, which is what I think theories should do to our minds.)

My catch-all sentence has it that literature offers us images to think with. Like all foolish sentences this one needs enlarging on, and there are three points about it I want to explore. They are about raw material, cleverness, and time machines.

Like every other creative activity, thinking requires raw material. I don't know about you, but I find I can never get enough raw material of my own. I take most of what I need from other people. On my own I am just not enough—in experience or knowledge or imaginative capacity or language. To put it another way round: thinking isn't really a self-contained, individual activity at all. It is a shared process. We are all members of the human think-tank.

Anyone who has done time in solitary confinement knows that's true. I speak from experience. I was in solitary a number of times. The prison authorities call it punishment; some kinds of monk call it their vocation. But there is an essential difference between the punitive and the vocational roles of solitary. The prison authorities do not let you talk to anyone in any way at all. Result: punishment. The monastic authorities do not let you speak to anyone but insist that you read the Bible. Result: refreshment. (The Bible, as some of you will recall, is a library of literature made up of stories, poems, and books of history, philosophy and biography.)

There is a phrase of C. S. Lewis's that sums this up. Through literature, he wrote, 'I become a thousand [people] and yet remain myself.' The prison authorities know that the worst you can do to people is not so much cut them off physically from each other, but cut them off from attempting to communicate their inner lives to each other—to throw them totally on to their own selves. While we can tell each other what is going on inside us and be told what is going on inside other people we remain human, sane, hopeful, creative. In short, we remain alive. Once storying stops, we are dead.

For this ex-monk who carried with him out of a monastery the profound experience of solitary confinement, the opening sentence of a great book still rings undeniably true, however it is interpreted by the reader. 'In the beginning was the Word, and the Word was with God, and the Word was God.' It is *with* words, *by* words, *through* words that we make sense of ourselves. And like any other great poetic novel, *The Gospel According to St John* provides enough raw material of such extraordinary richness that it never wears out, and helps us make and remake the most elaborate and resourceful of interior lives for ourselves.

That's all very well, some people say, if you're clever and advantaged; but literature is élitist. Recently I gave an open lecture on children's literature at a school of librarianship. [The Woodfield Lecture on p. 14.] Afterwards I received a letter from an unknown fan in the audience. He wrote: 'Dear Mr Chambers, I wanted to tell you what a complete waste of time your talk was . . . dealing with an industry which has very little impact on the lives of 90% of the population.'

Now my fan may have been right about the lecture, but he was quite wrong in his statistics. In some parts of the world children's literature has no impact on 100% of the population. In Britain the figure is about 60%. In some classrooms I know of, however, the percentage is demonstrably nil. In those places literature touches the lives of every person in the room every day they are there. So the first thing to say about the élitist argument is that literature itself isn't élitist. People make it so by a deliberate act of deprivation. If you do not believe in the importance of the literary act—or if you see that it is powerfully important and don't want other people to have that power—then you do not make financial or environmental provision for it, you do not build an educational system that places it at the centre, you do not make sure that literature in speech and print is cheaply and easily available.

Far from being élitist or accessible only to clever people, the truth about literature is that it is demotic. It is of the people. Literature— words in prose or verse which have for their purpose not the communication of fact but the telling of a story through the use of the inventive imagination in their employment (a formulation given by David Daiches in his *Critical Approaches to Literature*)—springs from our common humanity. One of the great things about it is that it can transcend human differences, like degrees of what we call cleverness, or social groups, or beliefs, or any of the other barriers, artificial and natural, that separate individuals.

Partly, the view that literature is élitist and good only for certain kinds of clever people comes from our over-valuing of particular kinds of literary works—those that tend to be lengthy and very complex in a self-consciously intellectual way—and a devaluing of short and apparently simple, less cerebral work. I yield to none, let me add, in the pleasure I take from long, complex, intellectually challenging literature. But this isn't the point. The point is that literature contains all, and is more profound *even at its simplest* than any other form of words.

Let's look at an example, and see some of what this can mean.

FOX AND COCK

Cock was sitting on a fence sunning himself.

Fox saw him. 'What a tasty meal Cock would be,' thought Fox. So he lay down behind a bush and waited for his chance.

'What a beautiful bird I am,' clucked Cock to himself. He smoothed his feathers and stuck out his chest. Then he crowed loudly to tell the world how grand he was.

Fox got up and trotted to the fence. 'Good morning, Cock,' he said. 'You are singing well today.'

'Thank you, Fox,' said Cock. 'I do have a fine voice, even if I say so myself.'

'Will you sing something just for me?' Fox asked.

'I would be glad to,' said Cock. He closed his eyes, threw back his head, and crowed loudly again.

Fox saw his chance. He sprang up, grabbed Cock by the throat, and ran off.

'Put me down!' shouted Cock. 'Help! Help!' he squawked.

The farmer heard Cock and saw what was happening.

'Stop, thief!' he cried, and chased after Fox.

All the farm animals heard the farmer shout and they followed him. The pigs, the cows, the geese, and, of course, all Cock's many hens.

'They are after you,' yelled Cock.

But Fox ran on. He knew he could run faster than any farm animal. Cock knew that too.

'Oh, Fox,' he said. 'What a runner you are! They will never catch you. You should tell them so.'

Fox felt pleased. He turned his head and called: 'You are too slow! This bird is mine!'

But when Fox opened his mouth, Cock flapped his wings and flew up into a tree.

Fox did not dare stop. He ran on into the wood.

'What a fool I am,' he said to himself. 'Sometimes it is better to keep your mouth shut!'

No need to say this is a version of an Aesop story.

One day some years ago a five-year-old boy who couldn't read heard that story and others from Aesop read aloud to him. He loved them at once. He would pore over the illustrations in the book for hours. He was a late developer and didn't learn to read fluently till he

7

was eight, and then he read Aesop stories for himself and liked them even more. Many years later, when he was asked to prepare some stories for people of six and seven, he knew at once which stories they had to be, because the pleasure they had given him when he was a non-reading six- and seven-year-old remained vividly with him. So he wrote his own versions of three of Aesop's tales about Fox and called the book *Fox Tricks*. (You do not have to be one of the Hardy boys or Nancy Drew to guess that the child I'm talking about was myself. Since those days, I've discovered the real problem in being a late developer: you develop too late.)

Here, then, we have proof of the fact that literature gives us images to think with, for that is what the Aesop stories did for that little boy. And as a late developer I have often in my lowest moments been comforted and encouraged by Aesop's stories, especially the one about the Tortoise and the Hare. (Incidentally, ever since hearing that tale, I have had an irrational and still so far unsatisfied desire to own a tortoise for a pet. Though, as I think about that confession now, I realize it is in itself another proof of literature's potential. It creates needs and desires in us that weren't there before.)

What I'd like to notice about *Fox and Cock*, however, is that here we have a story that could hardly be simpler. It takes about two minutes to read aloud, is 297 words in all. I now invite you to write down in no more than 300 equally simple words and equally simple sentences everything that's going on in it.

We all know better than to try. It would be pointless anyway, except as a special kind of exercise in literary criticism. We know we would fail because we know that in any literary use of language the words always mean more than they seem to say. Non-literary usage tries to say precisely and only what is meant. Literary language tries to do exactly the opposite, and even employs devices like irony so that one thing can be said when really something else is meant. A cussed way of going about things, but we enjoy it and find it useful.

In *Fox and Cock* we have a sequence of events concerning two animals, one of which is cunning and hungry, the other of which is self-congratulatory and seems also to be stupid. We see how flattery almost loses the stupid one its life and then saves it. Or is this a story that shows how wise reticence can be?

Then again, we know without anyone telling us, even when we are non-literary five-year-old late developers, that this story isn't actually about a couple of real live animals. It is, after all, only a story:

8

something a five-year-old late developer might say is just 'made up'. A lie, if you like. Yet any country child will also tell you foxes do behave rather as Fox does in the story, and cockerels can be very much like Cock. There is living truth in the story. The truth, then, in the guise of a lie; which means, therefore, this isn't a lie at all, but a form of the truth.

In any case, Aesop wasn't talking about animals, was he? We know this too. What then—or rather whom—was he talking about? People? We look around and, yes, we do notice people like Fox. When I was six his name was Peter Schofield; he was bigger than me and craftier. After hearing about Fox and Cock, I tried the flattery on him and it worked. I praised his jealously guarded Dinky toy collection and got to play with it as a result. Cock, for me, wasn't a boy but a woman. She lived three doors away and thought she was—I suppose the necessary image is—cock of the walk. I discovered that she simpered and went visibly weak at the knees when I flattered her, and that way got to have tea with her pretty daughter. I was not a late developer in everything.

Just a minute though. If you think about Fox and Cock differently, they aren't animals *or* people, specific or general. They are attributes. Parts of me. Aspects of humanity. I can get crafty when I'm hungry or can't have something I want very much. I'm capable of giving in to flattery and of using it as a weapon in my armoury for survival. So these fictional animals are really symbols of hunger and pride and cunning and flattery and the will to live, and are not creatures at all. Or rather, they are all those things at once. Animals, humans, attributes.

But we could, couldn't we?, go on like this for most of the morning. We could, for instance, discuss why we take such an interest in the fortunes of two fictional characters, why we sympathize with Fox but are glad Cock escapes his jaws, why we smile to ourselves all through the story, why the image of this unimportant fictional event remains in our memories, and has done in mine for over forty years and still somehow informs my life at unexpected and apparently unrelated moments. On and on.

I'm only rehearsing what we already know, so I'll add just one more strand to this layered network of meaning. Aesop's fable is all I've said it is, and yet is also nothing more than a few marks made with ink on paper. Of course, I might not know how to decipher those marks, but someone who has the skill and can speak can hand me Aesop's fable as it was first handed to me, as a gift of the tongue. This means of passing it on adds something and takes away something. But its essential nature remains, and reaches me, and can live in my memory.

In fact, I've arrived at the third of the points I said I wanted to make, the one about time machines. For literature in print transcends time and place and person. A book is a time-space machine: a three-dimensional object that has shape, weight, texture, smell, even taste. And compressed into those abstract marks made on pages it carries, by a mystery we still do not understand, a cargo of the deepest knowings of one person delivered directly to the most secret life of another, who may be many hundreds of miles away and many years of time distant too. Aesop was a Greek slave whose tales are often versions of stories told in India and Greece long before his time, and whose fables can still affect a very different man living two thousand miles from Aesop's home and two thousand five hundred years after his death. And this ancient form of storytelling continues so lively and strong that a book of newly invented stories of a similar kind can win a major prize—*Fables* by Arnold Lobel, recipient of the U.S. Caldecott Medal for 1981—and attract a writer of the absurd abilities of James Thurber, who adopts it for utterly twentieth-century purposes in his *Fables for Our Time*, in which the jokes depend on the reader being familiar with Aesop.

I hope I've made my point. What we can do with ourselves is limited by what we can do with our language. What a society does with literary language is the limit of what that society does for its people as a whole.

Language is a condition of being human; literature is a birthright. Entering into this birthright requires that every child be born into an environment that makes its birthright available, accessible, a gift to be desired.

So much for the beans; now for the instructions for getting into the can. Again, my task today is simply to rehearse what we all know so that our discussions can continue against a common background.

For my part, I find it useful to keep in mind that Reading Circle we are trying to set spinning and spiralling in the lives of our children. It looks like the diagram on the next page.

We cannot read anything until we have selected something to read. Our Western environment, at least, is already swamped with offers. Signs, adverts, newspapers, magazines, instruction labels, porno-

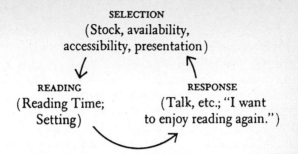

SELECTION
(Stock, availability,
accessibility, presentation)

READING
(Reading Time;
Setting)

RESPONSE
(Talk, etc.; "I want
to enjoy reading again.")

graphy, government forms, business documents . . . on and on. And in Britain alone something like 35,000 new books a year, about 3,000 of which are for children.

The principal responsibility, therefore, of those charged with power to bring children and books together is to put before children those literary works we consider most worth their time and attention. This responsibility has obvious implications for book stocks, their presentation, availability, and the opportunities we build into a child's day for browsing among books, so that children learn to choose for themselves.

But there is little point in spending time, money, and effort in providing books and making selections from them, if we never actually read any. Reading takes time. The more accomplished we become and the older we grow in childhood the more time and concentration literary reading demands. Indisputably, therefore, Time to Read, and settings which encourage and sustain that activity, are an essential element in every child's daily life. And the cold fact is that only in school can most children be ensured of that time and setting.

It is psychologically impossible to read something without experiencing a response. We may fall asleep from boredom; but that is a response. In the best circumstances two things tend to happen.

When most people have enjoyed a piece of literature, their instinct is to talk about it with a friend. We like to explore what has happened to us by talking it through. Children quite often want to draw and paint or act out what they've felt. Some people want to sit down and write something similar themselves. I've forgotten who first said that most authors are only readers who wanted to emulate their favourite authors.

The second response that we're especially looking for from

children, because it helps set the reading circle spinning in a self-sustaining way, is the one that says, 'I enjoyed the experience of reading this book so much I want to have it again.' The reader returns to the shelves looking for another book to read. We're back again where we started, with selection.

So now we have a reading programme which, ideally, every child should take part in on most days of the year. Here it is in note form:

—Browsing among a wide-ranging stock of literature and making own-choices from it.

—Hearing an adult read aloud, for enjoyment's sake, from literature that is (1) old and familiar, (2) new, to the child, and just about right for now, and (3) new, to the child, and challenging because it is ahead of where the child is as a reader.

—Time to read for oneself undisturbed.

—A chance to respond to what has been read in company with other children and in various ways, but especially by talking with adults.

—A chance to consult with a trusted adult about what might be read.

—A chance to buy books for oneself.

Now we come to the nub of the matter. Non-reading children are made by non-reading adults. Our resources may be poor, our stocks battered and too thin, we may be subject to all manner of difficulty. But one fact overrides all. The adult who reads for him/herself with conviction and who is knowledgeable about what is available for children is indispensable in literary education.

Indeed, such a person is so important that his/her active presence can succeed in the face of enormous problems to a point far in excess of a school that has much better facilities but lacks a reading adult. The evidence for this is now legion. But check, if you need to, in The Bullock Report, *A Language for Life*, in the Whitehead report, *Children's Reading Interests*, and see what Margaret M. Clark says in *Young Fluent Readers*.

Best of all, though, read *Cushla and her Books* by Dorothy Butler. Or perhaps I should say reread, for I doubt whether there is anyone in this room who has not been moved by the story of Cushla Yeoman. Cushla demonstrates in her life everything I've been trying to say here. Language formed her; indeed it was language that first woke her to the world against everything that the medical experts said could happen. It was language in books on which she grew to know the world she could hardly see or hear for herself. It was hearing language read aloud, and sung too, from books held almost literally at the end of her nose that taught her how to read for herself. Literature without any doubt gave Cushla Yeoman images to think with, and now she is a lively child able to live with spirit and joy against every adversity a damaged chromosome and a distressingly disabled body could put in her way.

But she has done it, and literature helped, only because there were adults around her who knew what had to be done and did it, often against the advice of expert opinion and gloomy prognosis.

Cushla takes away the question from that title: Libraries for All? She makes it a statement of universal need and determination. And so I'd like to finish by reading you what Dorothy Butler, Cushla's grandmother, says in the Postscript to her book [p. 107].

Seven years ago, before Cushla was born, I would have laid claim to a deep faith in the power of books to enrich children's lives. By comparison with my present conviction this faith was a shallow thing. I know now what print and picture have to offer a child who is cut off from the world, for whatever reason. But I know also that there must be another human being, prepared to intercede, before anything can happen. Had she been born to other parents— however intelligent and well-intentioned—Cushla might never have encountered, as a baby, word and picture between the covers of a book. Certainly, no authority prescribes reading aloud for chronically ill babies whose handicaps are thought to be mental as well as physical.

It is in the hope of recruiting more human links between books and the handicapped children of the world that Cushla's parents have agreed to the publication of her story. We are confident that a much older Cushla will want to help with this recruitment. We think that Cushla's belief in books as bridges may be even stronger than ours.

Axes
for Frozen Seas

The Woodfield Lecture is arranged annually by the Department of Library and Information Studies at Loughborough University under the sponsorship of Woodfield and Stanley Ltd, library suppliers and publishers of *Junior Bookshelf*, in honour of H. J. B. Woodfield, founder of the firm and the journal. 'Axes for Frozen Seas' was the fourth lecture, given in 1981. One of the more useful results of being asked to give a formal talk on a subject of your own choice is the chance to concentrate on topics of particular personal concern.

During the 1960s I had argued that more attention should be paid to children's immediate reading interests, that we should respect their views and taste, that we should publish more books that spoke directly to them. I had written *The Reluctant Reader* to support this line of thought in relation to fiction for teenagers, and had become general editor of the Topliners series in an attempt to do something about providing a publishing opportunity.

By the middle of the 1970s, however, I was sometimes dismayed by the turn the argument had taken. I had been saying that we needed the best of all kinds of literature and that some kinds were missing or were only done ineffectually. In other words I was arguing for a healthy, egalitarian pluralism. By the mid 1970s some people seemed to be suggesting that the only literature that mattered was whatever young people immediately liked. The litmus test was no longer the judgement of a particular group of adults from a literary background—whether they had anything to do with children or not (the group I had often criticized for their exclusive control over children's book publishing)—and was quickly shifting to the judgement of groups of adults with other special interests (to do with, for instance, racism, politics, sexism, commercial bookselling and like preoccupations), who always claimed to be working on behalf of children's own opinions and 'rights'. These care-takers often made a near-fetish of selecting books according to two criteria: first, whether the book met the demands of their own specialist point of view (if it was 'positive' in its depiction of, say, sex roles, or would sell in large quantities if book-ownership was the aim); and, second, whether on an untutored reading children instantly liked the book.

The pendulum had swung from an élitist to an equally narrow, populist extreme. Underlying this shift was a changed assumption about the role of the teacher, expressed in slogans like 'The teacher should not impose his/her own tastes on children'. The modish word was 'intervention'. Should the teacher ever intervene between children and their reading was a seriously asked question. The old-fashioned attitude held that children learned to be discriminating readers by being given only the best of great literature and being shown by discriminating teachers how to read it. The new view was that children became discriminating readers by reading anything and everything they wanted to and so learned to decide for themselves what they preferred, the terms 'good' and 'bad' literature being suspect.

I found myself in agreement with neither extreme. I saw books of extraordinary character being ignored by influential adults simply because of their oddity or difference from some popular norm and therefore never finding their way to children, who, as a result, got no chance at all to decide whether they liked them or not. While the important question of how a teacher helps children enjoy what at first sight seem 'difficult' books was seldom discussed or was dismissed as irrelevant.

All this came to a head for me when *The Stone Book* by Alan Garner was published in 1976. In the next few years I grew tired of being told by teachers that children didn't like it, that they didn't think it was a children's book at all. I knew from my own experience that, given some help, children could find it one of the most stimulating books available. Other teachers worked with me in bringing it to young readers, often confirming my own findings, and helping in the discovery of how to read this exceptional work and how to present it to our pupils.

When the invitation came to give the Woodfield Lecture, therefore, I knew what I wanted to do. I wanted to say something about what I had come to think of as 'transformational' writing. I meant quite simply literature which, if read creatively, reader and author making the story together, had the effect of transforming us as

15

readers and as people. I had already tried to explore this from a critical point of view in 'The Reader in the Book' (p. 34). Now I wanted to demonstrate it through the words of other teachers and their pupils as they reported such readings to me.

The version given here has been slightly edited and begins after the pleasantries customary on such an occasion.

*

Before I tell you about the passage from which my title comes, I must try your patience with an autobiographical titbit. It is twenty-five years this academic year since I began work bringing literature and children together. In all that time some thoughts have remained constant, some aims primary. Forgive me for stating them again; I'll be brief.

First, it is my conviction, strengthening as the years go by, that literary reading is the single most important cultural and educational activity we all—adults and children—engage in. Second, literary reading begins where the reader is and goes on from there. Unless you find yourself in books you have a hard time finding anybody else. Third, the presence of plenty of books, wide-ranging in story and treatment, the chance to browse among them frequently, to hear them read aloud, and being given time to read them for oneself, are all central to children's literary development. Fourth, we learn more and more certainly every year that the mediation of literature to children by a literate, sympathetic adult is the single most important factor in the creation of a desire among children to read, and to read adventurously—a point I shall come back to later.

I repeat all this here because I am conscious that what I want to say in the rest of this talk might easily be misunderstood. So let me reinforce the point. I belong to the demotic tradition; I believe literature belongs to all the people all the time, that it ought to be cheaply and easily available, that it ought to be fun to read as well as challenging, subversive, refreshing, comforting, and all the other qualities we claim for it. Finally, I hold that in literature we find the best expression of the human imagination, and the most useful means by which we come to grips with our ideas about ourselves and what we are.

Which brings me to those frozen seas. The phrase comes from a letter written by Franz Kafka when he was twenty years old to his friend Oskar Pollack. They were debating the ancient argument

16

about whether literature is simply a diversion, a way of spending time happily, or whether it has some greater value. This is what Kafka wrote:

> It seems to me that one should only read books which bite and sting one. If the book we are reading does not wake us up with a blow on the head, what's the point of reading? To make us happy, as you write to me? Good God, we would be just as happy without books, and books which make us happy, we can at a pinch write them for ourselves. On the other hand we have need of books which act upon us like a misfortune from which we would suffer terribly, like the death of someone we are fonder of than ourselves ... a book must be the axe which smashes the frozen sea within us. That's what I think. [p. 12]

Kafka's images are bleak, and for my part I must say at once that I can't for the life of me see why we shouldn't have what both men want. I don't want just some kinds of literature; I want it all. On the other hand, I do have to say that in the end Kafka is right. If literature doesn't do for us what he wants, it isn't worth bothering about. Indeed, if all I am looking for is diversion I can always get it with far less effort than reading costs from television and films, or, best of all, from doing nothing. I am not very interested—and never have been—in bringing children up as diversionary readers. I have always assumed that the idea was to bring children into their literary heritage, and to enable them in the act of the deepest possible and most avidly desired literary reading.

I must admit that recently I've begun to feel that if most people responsible for bringing literature and children together used to think that this was the central aim, a great many think it is the case no longer. An admired and popular poet for children told me the other day that he doesn't regard himself as a poet—which is entirely his affair of course—and that he didn't think it mattered whether or not children ever read any of the poets from our past. One rather stark example of what I mean. Another, I note with some depression, is that a number of publishers have cut almost to nothing their production of children's novels, except for the predictably popular, and have increased the kind of non-literary publishing they do: the pop-up toys which are books only because they are bound between covers; the gimmick books, the obvious example of which must be

Masquerade (an admirably apt title in the circumstances); and the promotion of routine adventure stories, thin in every sense, as something virtuous because they are, as the saying goes, what children want.

In fact, the thing that now worries me most is an attitude not just visible but, to use a word of the stockmarket and one which is again apt in the circumstances, bullish. It is fashionable just now to assume—not to argue or suggest but to assume—that what children want are books which have an immediate undifferentiated appeal, that they must be either funny or pertinent, by which is usually meant, the subject must be one that is a preoccupation of the adult concerned. Complexity, multi-layering, richness of language, the kind of book which demands that the reader match the author in an act of creation that costs thought and energy: these are out-of-date.

Before I go on—a last attempt to keep my balance in your ears— let me say that I too look for books that have immediate appeal, that amuse me, and that deal with subjects I want to hear about. And I am *not* someone who claims that the *children* in children's literature don't matter. On the contrary. It is because they matter so much that Kafka's demand for literature that transforms—if I may use that word to contain the ideas behind what he was saying and what I'm trying to say too—currently needs reasserting and indeed reassessing in our thinking about literature and children.

Perhaps I should try and identify more closely the sort of book I have in mind when I talk about transformation. Books that transform me as I read, and go on working in me afterwards when they have become part of me, often refresh and reinvigorate the language. At the very least they attend to it. Words are what an author uses. In one sense they are all s/he uses. Thus literature is, among other things, about words, about language. Whether you are like Philippa Pearce, who wants to write in such a way that the reader feels s/he can reach through the book like reaching through a window and touch what is on the other side—an aim George Orwell owned as well—or whether you are like James Joyce, who clearly wanted his readers to feel the weight and quality of his language on the page, you cannot escape language either as an author or as a reader.

Then the transforming books are ones which, as W. H. Auden says in his marvellously lucid essay, 'Reading', 'can be read in a number of different ways. Vice versa, the proof that pornography has no literary value is that, if one attempts to read it in any other way than as a sexual stimulus, to read it, say, as a psychological case-history of the author's sexual fantasies, one is bored to tears.'

Transformational books enrich in some degree our image of the world and its being; they help illuminate me, and others for me, and the society I live in, as well as the societies other people live in.

To try and boil all that down: the transforming books are multi-layered, multi-thematic, linguistically conscious, dense. The opposite sort of writing is—to use another catch–all word for convenience' sake—reductionist. By which I mean it limits what we read to a narrow range of the familiar, the obvious, the immediately appealing, and concentrates on subjects and treatments confined to the bland and well-tried.

All of which sounds excessively ponderous and solemn, as if I think transformational books are always likely to be obscure and difficult. On the contrary, as I hope to demonstrate in a minute.

Before that, two more points. First, happily there are signs in more and more schools that we are beginning to take seriously the idea that children are quite as capable as adults of critical reading—in the literary sense—and that we need to understand more about how to engage with them in critical responses. Second, we are perhaps beginning to appreciate also that creating literary readers is a matter of raising expectations in the reader that match the demands of the book in question. I have, for example, heard adults tell children that Lucy Boston's *Children of Green Knowe* is a ghost story. That is a case of raising the wrong expectations and there can be no wonder that children find the book boring or confusing and don't finish reading it, if that is what they are led to expect.

These points in mind, let me go on to some books, beginning with *The Crane* by Reiner Zimnik. It has had a chequered history. First published by Brockhampton Press (now Hodder) in 1969 in a translation from the original German by Marion Koenig, it had what is usually described as a modest success. In other words, no one paid much attention. Later, it appeared in a Puffin edition using the U.S. translation published by Harper and Row, which cuts out significant elements. I doubt if that version fared any better. My attention was drawn to the book when Nancy published in the September 1971 issue of *Signal* an article by Nina Danischewsky, which did for me what I hope to find all the time in critical writing. Let me list what I mainly look for in criticism. I hope critics will:

1. Introduce me to authors or works of which I was hitherto unaware.
2. Convince me that I have undervalued an author or a work because I had not read them carefully enough.
3. Show me relations between works of different ages and cultures which I could never have seen for myself because I do not know enough and never shall.
4. Give a 'reading' of a work which increases my understanding of it.
5. Throw light upon the process of artistic 'Making'.
6. Throw light upon the relation of art to life, to science, economics, ethics, religion, etc.

Of course I did not compile this list; you'll find it in the essay by W. H. Auden I referred to earlier, which is included in *The Dyer's Hand* [p. 8]. Danischewsky's article covered numbers 1 to 4. Pretty good going in one piece. I'm still grateful to her for that service, and expect to remain so. Zimnik's work is, in my view, one of the small masterpieces of children's literature.

The Crane is deceptively direct in tone, plain and simple in the folk-tale manner, but I began to realize with Danischewskian hindsight that it is also laden with challenges and the features I described earlier as belonging to transformational work. Child characters enter the story only incidentally. The protagonist is, at the beginning, a young workman who wears a feather in his blue cap. He is given the job of driving the town's new crane—the tallest in the country— climbs to the cabin and there remains, attended from below by his friend, the dreamer Lektro, who drives an electric delivery truck.

During the story, as episodic events are related to us, weeks pass and years; even, one sometimes feels, social epochs. Certainly we witness a war, an elemental flood, a repopulation of the earth. But through it all the crane driver stays at his post, a survivor, a witness, a prophetic figure, and a fool in the classic sense. The variety of interpretive possibilities, Zimnik's textual manner, the absence of child characters, and the unapologetic refusal of the text to hide its indeterminacies behind a façade of persuasive explanatory detail have confused, even disturbed, so many adult readers that the book has often been judged 'unsuitable' for children, too difficult, too strange.

The fiction is all the more opaque for these readers because of other devices also. Zimnik's omniscient narrator will, for instance, enter the story from time to time, moving from the third person to the first. 'I have drawn the town councillors flat on purpose' he suddenly announces on the story's fourth page, and if you look at the illustration you see he has indeed done just that. This text detail was one of those cut out of the American version, even though it is a crucial element in the success of the narrative. The line drawings that share the book half-and-half with the words similarly play about with point of view, with the openly fictional set against a pretence of the realistic. They include, for instance, documentary realia like the facsimile of a telegram sent to the crane driver and drawings of fish with holes in their bodies swimming happily about.

In words and drawings, between which there is a subtle and generative relationship, for both are needed to make the Text, the images are placed one after another without specific linking by way of connections suggested by the narrator, or the usual conventions of story logic. So, from readers with closed minds about how narrative should work, the book gets short shrift.

But Zimnik is not trying for the kind of narrative consistency familiar in most children's stories. What he is doing is closer to dream narrative. As in dream, the images present themselves as entirely inevitable. We must first accept them like that, as individual images each with its own meaning, and not struggle to find a logic connecting one to the next. Zimnik helps us by employing an oral storyteller's style: concrete, uncluttered, simple in diction and syntax (or at least that is how the translation is and we must suppose it is true to the original). Not only does this style produce the naturalistic surface Zimnik wants, but it also connects with children. He can be fairly sure that children, if they know any narrative modes at all, are most likely to be familiar with the folk-fairy tale. He can therefore hope to draw child readers in, getting them on his side, by the comfortable familiarity of his narrative's codes and language. Here is a sample:

The crane grew taller every day and the men working at the top strapped themselves on with safety-belts. Every afternoon, after five o'clock, crowds came out of the town to stroll past the structure and they all said:
'It's going to be a marvellous crane,' and the children—and most of the men—were very proud of the crane.

There was one workman who loved the crane more than anybody else did. He was young and had a feather in his blue cap and he

loved the crane so much that they all said: 'He's out of his mind.'
He hammered and riveted three times faster than the other men,
and when they went home at the end of the day, he climbed around
at the top of the crane polishing all the screws with his handker-
chief until they shone. Every night he slept under the crane. And
every morning he jumped in and out of its shadow while all the
others said: 'That man with the feather in his blue cap is out of his
mind.' [pp. 14, 15]

In this beguiling way we are offered scenes, episodes, the structural point being not that they make step-by-step sense in the way
that naturalistic convention dictates, but that each presents a possible
meaning in itself, which, when taken with the possible meanings of
each of the other scenes in the book, build up to a sequence of related
meanings rather than a sequence of related events leading to a
conclusive meaning. Besides this, or along the way, we get scenes of
comic extravagance, of poignance, of almost Kafka-esque bleakness
and loss. The effect is emotional in quality, not intellectual. If you try
thinking about the story as you go along, it becomes impossibly
obscure. Afterwards is the time for sorting it out. Another problem,
this, for many English literary readers, whose training has taught
them to read with their heads and to naturalize every page as they go
along. But I'd suggest that the kind of reading *The Crane* calls for is
much closer to a naïve child's way of reading than it is to the trained
adult's, which rejects *The Crane* as too puzzling or too difficult.

There is some interesting evidence to support that view. Robert
Wintle, a teacher in a Bristol comprehensive school, works with
twelve- and thirteen-year-olds who need remedial help. This is what
he wrote to me about his children's response to *The Crane*:

When I started reading aloud—without any introduction or
explanation—they became extremely attentive. Next day they
were anxious for the story to be continued. I was also asked to 'just
read the story and not stop to explain anything'—such as difficult
words. I was fortunate in being able to use the last lesson of most
afternoons to read to the class. A further bonus was that the room
was a newly converted cloakroom, which, having a concrete floor,
had been carpeted wall to wall, as the cheapest form of floor
covering. The class of sixteen children soon developed a routine of
their own. The desks and chairs were arranged around me so that

each child was able to sit comfortably in the semicircle. Some sat on the floor and some sat beside me so that they could see the pictures. Although this is accepted as a norm in primary schools, it was very unusual behaviour for a whole class of children of this age in my school.

At suitable places in the text I held up the book and showed it around the group—quickly, so that the relevant pictures and passages could be matched. The group were extremely attentive, and they were obviously listening with quiet enjoyment. There was an almost tangible rapport with the class when reading to them, which made the experience mutually pleasurable.

When the story was finished, I was surprised that they requested me to read it again. The same ritual with the furniture again took place, but this time they requested a good look at certain pictures which they apparently felt were important for an understanding or interpretation. There was also some discussion on the nature of the town councillors, for example, and also what the children thought was really happening in the story. Naturally enough, they rapidly picked up the points giving insight into human nature or behaviour, although the deeper layers of meaning in the story were not obviously apparent to them. Nevertheless, the mystical and surrealistic elements evoked the greatest enjoyment—for example, the passages about the silver lion, and the eagle. These were the passages which they enjoyed hearing and which seemed to touch a chord—evoke the greatest response—although naturally enough it was not possible for them to put their feelings into words.

The interest in the book was maintained for some weeks, with intense pleasure.

I find Robert's account both moving and impressive. Anyone who has done 'remedial' work with children of pubescent age will know how alienated from literature of any but the most immediately enjoyable kind they have been made, how short a span of concentration their stamina can sustain. Yet here is a group whose interest *The Crane* stimulated for 'some weeks', and there are features one wants to note. The way, for example, the environment helped—the carpet, Bob's allowing the group to adopt a natural and comfortable physical relation to himself, the book, and each other. (When will we learn that what is true in the early years is just as true right through secondary school where reading is concerned?) The fact that he began without raising any expectations at all is interesting: the adult *not* getting in the way beforehand, for once. Maybe we try too hard too often, and don't trust the book to do its own work.

Nor is Bob Wintle's experience rare. I've heard from a teacher of a class of mixed-ability top juniors, for example, who listened to a serial reading with the same attention as Bob's thirteen-year-olds and who, at the end, stood up and cheered in a spontaneous outburst of applause the teacher told me he had never before witnessed in a classroom. Yet another teacher experienced just the opposite: a total silence she dared not break because it was the silence of an emotion too fragile to speak about.

Yet the continuing history of this book is far from what these reports would lead one to expect. Because I saw it disappearing into the land of O.P., from which few volumes ever return, I persuaded Macmillan to publish the Hodder translation in M Books, the fiction list of educational editions which I edit. From the beginning *The Crane* has been one of the very few poor sellers. Given the experience of teachers like Bob Wintle, one wonders, a little gloomily, why this is so.

Partly, I think, it has to do with the mediating adults raising the wrong expectations, or—much more likely—not themselves being able to sort out what a book possesses. Charles Keeping's work is another case in point. I rushed into one of my local children's libraries recently needing a Keeping picture book for some work I was doing. The librarian said, 'Oh yes, we've got it of course, and it will be on the shelf. Keeping isn't very popular.' Confident of her words, she took me to the stacks. Not one copy of any Keeping was there . 'Typical!' she said. And indeed that sort of thing does happen just when you least expect it. But I fancy she was unconsciously parading the received opinion about Keeping's subtler picture books: that they aren't children's books because their artwork is too sophisticated. This isn't a view held by Jill Hopes, a teacher of infants in a Swindon school. She wrote to me:

When I consider the hundred or more picture books I have in my room . . . in most of them the author/artist's intentions are quite clear-cut. But Keeping leaves gaps for the imagination to fill in a very definite way and in a manner which infants do not often experience . . . Keeping uses colour actually to set the scene for strong emotions . . . His books usually carry obscure meanings, which children have to be encouraged to find. He makes no concessions to age, and one of the strongest features of his books—and, I believe, an invaluable one—is the depth of the texts. They are usually sparsely worded but with an extension of language which is unusual in picture books. A general criticism made of Keeping seems to be that children will not understand his books. Young children understand more than we give them credit for.

I asked Jill to show me somehow the truth of that. What I got back was not another letter but a book, called *A Book All About Books*, made for me by her six-year-olds, and all about Keeping, accompanied by a cassette of the children talking about their reading of *Charley, Charlotte and the Golden Canary*, of *Joseph's Yard* and the rest. Jill says in her covering note: 'After a fortnight of almost pure Charles Keeping, I did wonder yesterday whether I had overdone it, as when talking of the recent assassination attempt in America [against President Reagan], I asked for the name of the president. It was not forthcoming, so I said, "Come on, who is one of the most powerful and important men in the world?" Lee answered immediately and with great confidence, "Charles Keeping".'

Here are just two of the children's responses to Keeping from their book about him, sentences extracted from surprisingly long accounts, considering the ages of the children:

CHRISTOPHER: The pictures look like when I dream because they are scribbly and you can see the shape but they do not look really real.

LEE: When Charley found Charlotte with the golden canary, I felt happy and I don't like losing my friends because Craig was my friend and he has gone to the Isle of Wight and I miss him and feel sad.

On and on through this lovely book: six-year-olds as critics, and enjoying themselves enormously. Open, intelligent, their experience of reading books some say are too difficult for them captured in their own words and drawings. Would that adult critics and reviewers could be so direct, so honest, and so ready to allow a book to shape their lives. I cherish especially one sentence heard on Jill's tape. One of the girls was talking of losing her friend Kevin; she finished by saying with sudden brightness, 'But I've still got Kevin in my head.' Surely this is a transformation, a coming to conscious understanding of experience, that has resulted from her reading of Keeping's fiction about *Charley, Charlotte and the Golden Canary*. An axe for a frozen sea all right!

There is a critical path to be followed in all our reading, and in our work with children, if the ice is to be broken at all. In reading we pass through a sequence of time-space warps. If we aren't allowed to, the books always remain one surface, one time. We never then discover the narrative layers and the pleasure we get in finding them. To do that we have to stay in the time-space capsule long enough.

Here is another teacher, Irene Suter, head of a junior school in Wiltshire, doing just that with her children—letting them travel for long enough. Rene has converted her office into a mini-library. Every afternoon she has children with her in groups numbering up to eight, never more, for twenty minutes to half an hour each group. This way she sees every child in the school once every three weeks or so and, in that environment, reads and talks informally with them. She has been watching especially what happens to Anthony Browne's books, and has recorded for me the spontaneous comments made by these five-to eleven-year-olds when she showed them *A Walk in the Park* for the first time, and then showed them it again later. Rene wrote:

The first stage always seems to be like a detective game—a puzzle-solving: How many absurdities can you find? Already, though, more profound questions are emerging, questions that relate to layers of meaning, inner meaning, pictorial jokes, pictorial representation of ideas, or social implications, or emotional differences, styles of living, the narrow dividing line between reality and fantasy, and the disturbing notion that not all experiences can be accounted for logically. Those more profound questionings seem to be more obvious at a second reading.

I think that books like Anthony Browne's engage children in exploring, from a very early age, ideas such as:
a. there may be other meanings in a text than are at first apparent—layers of meaning;
b. there may be additional parts of a story, not contained in the text, which are apparent only in illustrations;
c. that illustrations themselves can have several layers of meaning;

d. that you can have a practical joke [in a book];

e. that humour may be found in a joke that uses both words and a picture, when the latter has an essential part to play, not merely to illustrate a text;

f. that question-posing, arising from the text or illustrations, can lead to the discovery of additional meanings;

g. that speculation aroused by apparent incongruity can lead to exploration of response beyond the anecdotal or character-exploring stages;

h. that books demand a contribution from the reader;

i. that meaning in a text or picture is not always self-evident, or so simplistic as to be unarguable, and that each meaning is derived only by an individual response, and can be different from one individual to another.

Typical of the first-reading comments Rene recorded are these:

'That flower's got a face!'

'Hey, look at that hedge. It's her! It's the lady—Mrs Smythe.'

'There's an apple on the top there—is it real?'

'What's funny here? It's the trees—look, that's getting thicker—like a tree coming into leaf.'

During the second reading the conversation is more like this:

'What's that Mickey Mouse? Is he real?'
'No, he's just a toy.'
'He could be waving goodbye to them.'
'Not if he isn't real.'
'Anyway, what is a real Mickey Mouse?'
'I think that Smudge is just thinking about him.'

'It's a funny park! It's all dark in the wood. It's not like a real park at all.'
'I think it's a dream.'
'It must be a dream—nobody takes pigs for a walk!'
'You could—I suppose.'
'Not likely. Anyway, you'd never see Tarzan and Father Christmas together—not even on TV.'

'You might in a story.'

'Yes, but this is a story—already!'

'Yes, I know—I mean, I could write a story with them both in.'

'But this story—the words—don't say anything about them.'

I hope you'll accept from these samples what Rene Suter claims for Browne's book and its effect on children. As well, her recording shows what can be done, where the talk can go, provided two things: that the opportunities are created for such talk; and that books which generate such response are put before young readers. Another point: as Rene herself is discovering and saying, we haven't begun to tackle the possibilities there are in talking with children about literature because we haven't studied carefully enough how to handle what children say about what they read. At least Rene is taking the first crucial step: she is listening carefully to what they say and is letting those cues guide her work.

Before I move on, though, let me quote another snatch of these children's conversations. 'I see a rainbow,' one child said. 'It's not a rainbow. It's like my painted one,' said her friend. 'What's it doing there anyway?' said the first child. 'Well,' said the other, 'rainbows is happy things. That's why it's there.'

Rene's work is admirable. So too was a project reported to me by Barbara Telford, a young teacher who works in a junior school in Swindon. She read *The Stone Book* by Alan Garner and found, she wrote, that

I have never been involved with any written material before which raised quite as many emotive reactions [in myself]. The family aspects drew me in. It is now seven years since I finally left my parents' home to build a life of my own. This summer was the first time that I returned by myself as a daughter not as a daughter and wife. I found myself thinking about the effect my 'roots' have had on my present life and status. I actually stayed at my grandmother's house and helped in a major redecorating scheme which obliterated many of the visual images left from my childhood staying at that house. The sense of destroying evidence from the past was very strong as the character of half the house was changed beyond recognition. Looking at a photograph of my great-grand-parents that fell off the wall, I saw them for the first time as being ancestors of mine, and not just my mother's ancestors. I did not believe it possible that I should be secretly perturbed by a modernization scheme. This heightened awareness of the past has emerged in other situations. I have never been interested in history. I have always regarded antique bric-à-brac as rubbish. Old furniture has always been ugly and dirty, in my view. Now I find old things more attractive, as I try to place them with the people that may have used them . . .

The Stone Book has certainly been an axe smashing a frozen sea in the life of that young teacher. And, what is best, she knows it, and is prepared to say so. Under that personally transforming impetus, she took the four books of *The Stone Book* quartet to her class of eight- and nine-year-olds. Her comments acknowledge the difficulties she faced. Her children's appreciation of literature was, as she put it, embryonic. And at the time she was gripped by *The Stone Book*, the general professional opinion was that children wouldn't and didn't like it. Not a children's book at all, some said forcefully.

Barbara's very long record of what happened next is full of insights into what it means to bring transformational literature to children. Here is a flavour of this impressive teaching:

By having the confidence to allow the children a free hand in a class discussion, aspects of the narrative had to be thrashed out and understood by the group. They were not always given the answers on a plate and very often the children introduced inter-pretations that I had not previously realized. As a teacher, this is a lesson that I must bear in mind, as I tend to oversteer and restrict channels of thought and imagination . . . Yet another warning to me to concentrate more on *what the children say* and less on what *I* am going to say next to keep the group on my own train of thought.

Barbara writes as if she alone made these mistakes, needing to learn these lessons. If she could read a number of transcripts of class discussions of books, and sit, as I have to quite often, and listen to adults talk with children about books, she would realize that what she is discovering is what most of us still need to be more aware of.

Most impressive of all to me is Barbara's range of approaches. She sorted out what the book asks of a reader who wants to enter into it to the fullest possible extent, and found child-appropriate ways of making those connections with her children. They climbed their local church tower, for example, to compare their experience with Mary's in *The Stone Book*. (She had to resist a demand that they climb the tower, like Mary, on the outside!) They devised a family tree for the characters in the quartet and then made their own family trees—with, I might add, amusing results in the relationships they discovered among their class. They brought into school treasured family objects—those items of bric-a-brac rubbish Barbara once despised—and found themselves making an exhibition of quite startling variety and interest, the artefacts grouping themselves primarily around First World War mementoes and stuff brought back from the old British Empire in the days when Britannia spread her red across the map: unexpectedly tangible evidence of the deep-seated influence of those two threads in British life still active in the homes of ordinary folk in an English industrial town. They wrote, drew, played games stimulated by Garner's story; and in doing all this, experienced *The Stone Book* itself in at least two full readings, as well as a recording of the author reading it himself, and a viewing of his TV *Writer's Workshop* programme on the background to the writing of the story.

Ending her account, Barbara says, 'I did not feel bored once . . . never once did I drag my feet on the way back to the classroom after break. On the contrary, trying to work through this project caused me many anxious moments as the time available became more and more curtailed as we approached the end of term. This left timing of the reading sessions rather awkward.' She had, she writes, under-estimated 'the length of time needed and the quantity of content in the quartet. "I never knew there was so much in it," ' she joked, quoting a *TV Times* advertisement of that year, concluding, 'We did, after all, spend six weeks on only four relatively short texts.'

Of course there were moments when her children felt weary, moments when they said this was a boring bit. But instead of running for cover, wanting only immediate success and the sense of achievement a teacher can get from the easy business of making children roll about in laughter, she stuck by her enthusiasm, her belief in the worth of the book she was handling, and the value of the time spent, and indeed a belief that in the end her children would thank her for it. They did thank her for it, and there can be little doubting that, in the six summer weeks of this experience, their approach to a work of literature was itself transformed.

Of the books I've mentioned so far, *The Stone Book* best exemplifies the features I began by outlining. Its consciousness of language, the layered density of the narrative, the freshness of its approach to people and events, its structuring, its simplicity, and (the most subtle, least discussed aspect, even among people like myself who admire the book greatly) the fact that it is not the straightforward, sequentially controlled and naturalistic story it pretends to be: all these things make it a touchstone by which to redefine the limits and possibilities of literature for the young.

Of course Garner's reputation guaranteed considerable attention for the quartet, whatever the judgements reached when it came out. Quoting Auden again:

> We cannot read an author for the first time in the same way that we read the latest book by an established author. In a new author, we tend to see either only his virtues or only his defects and, even if we do see both, we cannot see the relation between them. In the case of an established author, if we can still read him at all, we know that we cannot enjoy the virtues without tolerating the defects we deplore. Moreover, our judgement of an established author is never simply an aesthetic judgement. In addition to any literary merit it may have, a new book by him has a historic interest for us as the act of a person in whom we have long been interested. He is not only a poet or a novelist; he is also a character in our biography. [p. 4]

This being so, we should examine carefully how we arrive at our decisions about the books we bring to children, and the features of those books to which we direct children's attention. Let me, therefore, tell you the plot of my own reading.

The first question I ask is *not*, 'Will children like this book?' The first question, it seems to me, should be, 'What happens to me as I read this book?'

I am still surprised at how difficult it is for most children's-book professionals to disengage from an immediate attempt, as soon as they pick up a book, to put some representative child in front of them as they read. All this does is act as a barrier to their own understanding, and therefore to their assessment.

So first, read; and as I read I am, to use a crude image, tape-recording my response as I go. This sounds terribly self-conscious and wearying, but it isn't, once you're used to it.

My responses fall into two categories. First, there are those caused by some feature or other in the book calling up my history as a person. Thus, for example, any domestic death scene inevitably conjures numerous memories of my childhood spent as an undertaker's son. And this colours my reading; it has to be allowed for, set against what the book may be trying to evoke. And part of this personally based reaction is the response caused by my history as a reader. In other words, to some extent all books are made out of other books; and all reading is made or marred by our previous reading. These elements must be sorted out too. Sometimes an author will deliberately be playing on them, as, to take an obvious example, the Ahlbergs do with nursery tales and characters in *Each Peach Pear Plum*, and as Jane Austen makes use of her teenage reading of Gothic novels in *Northanger Abbey*. Sometimes a book cannot escape its literary antecedents whether it wants to or not, as is the case with David Storey's *Saville*, which cannot escape D. H. Lawrence's *Sons and Lovers*.

Already, then, there is the book I read as I was reading it for the first time, and a second book that results from my contemplation of that experience. Now we find a third book, the one that answers the question, 'How did the author make this book?' This is the sort of reading many of us were taught in secondary- and college-level English Lit. Some of us dislike it because of that drilling. I happen to have been taught by someone who made literary detective work enormously invigorating, so I still enjoy doing it. And it does help one understand what an author wants readers to meet in his/her work.

That done—and it sounds too pat and schematic; in fact, everything goes on in one's mind at once—the next question is, 'What does this book call for from a reader if s/he is to enjoy what it offers and to discover the book's potentialities?' It is at this point that talking with other readers makes the most sense. If you like, our talking begins with a sharing of enthusiasms. I like this bit, I didn't like that bit, how surprising that you noticed that and not this . . . and so on. It moves on to a sharing of problems. Why do you think the author did this? What does that mean? Why aren't we told about such-and-such? But at the heart of the exchange is always an attempt to discover the book the author was trying to make. So now we have a fourth book: the one that grows out of sharing experience and understanding.

While all this is going on we begin to see what we will need to do with children if they are to match themselves and this particular book, as Barbara Telford did with *The Stone Book*. We also find out the reference points a reader needs. Some may be too obscure for our children and then we'll know it might be better to lead up to this book through others that prepare the way—as, say, *Flat Stanley* happens to prepare the way for *The Shrinking of Treehorn*: they lie on the same track of narrative manner. We begin, in other words, to set the book up against the children, begin to answer the question, not 'Will children like this book?' but 1) Is this book worth children's time and attention? If so, 2) How do I best help them engage in it, and so enjoy it? We decide, from our understanding of the book, what expectations to raise in children about it, and how best to raise those expectations in the children who face us. We might here recall Robert Wintle's wisdom in letting the book do its own work sometimes, without the adult raising any expectations at all but simply acting as an enabler: the person who provides time, the right kind of reading environment, the books themselves, and the atmosphere in which to read them.

In the end, if literature for children is to act like axes smashing frozen seas, the hands that best wield those axes will belong to sympathetic and knowledgeable adults who wield for themselves, with enormous pleasure and skill, axes of their own size and weight.

The
Reader in the Book

This article is based on a talk, titled 'A Children's Book is for Children', given in February 1977 at the University of Bristol School of Education. First published in *Signal* 23, May 1977, and often reprinted and reproduced elsewhere, sometimes in strangely abridged versions, it received the first award for excellence in criticism given annually by the Children's Literature Association in the U.S.A.

I

1. Two to say a thing . . .

There is constant squabble about whether particular books are children's books or not. Indeed, some people argue that there is no such thing as books for children but only books which children happen to read. And unless one wants to be partisan and dogmatic—which I do not, having had my fill of both—one has to agree that there is some truth on both sides and the whole truth in neither.

The fact is that some books are clearly *for* children in a specific sense—they were written by their authors deliberately for children—and some books, never specifically intended for children, have qualities which attract children to them.

But we must go further than that truism, which helps us very little to deal critically with books or to mediate them intelligently and effectively. We need a critical method which will take account of the child-as-reader; which will include him rather than exclude him; which will help us to understand a book better and to discover the reader it seeks. We need a critical method which will tell us about the reader in the book.

For it seems to me that all literature is a form of communication, a way of saying something. Samuel Butler once observed that it takes two to say a thing, a sayee as well as a sayer—a hearer as well as a speaker. Thus, if literature is a way of saying something, it requires a reader to complete the work. And if this is so, as I am convinced it is, it must also be true that an author addresses someone as he writes. That someone has come to be called 'the implied reader'.

2. The implied reader

Let me defend myself against an obvious objection. I am not suggesting that, as an author writes, he necessarily has in the front of his mind a particular reader. F. H. Langman in a useful article, 'The Idea of the Reader in Literary Criticism', puts it this way:

> I do not say we need to know what readers the author had in mind. An author may write for a single person or a large public, for himself or for nobody. But the work itself implies the kind of reader to whom it is addressed and this may or may not coincide with the author's private view of his audience. What matters for the literary critic is to recognize the idea of the reader implied by the work. Not only correct understanding but also evaluation often depends principally upon correct recognition of the implied reader. [p. 84]

I would go further. I would say that, until we discover how to take account of the implied reader, we shall call fruitlessly for serious attention to be paid to books for children, and to children as readers by others than that small number of us who have come to recognize their importance. What has bedevilled criticism of children's books in the past is the rejection of any concept of the child-reader-in-the-book by those who have sought most earnestly for critical respect-ability. And they have done this, have set aside the reader-in-the-book, in the belief that mainstream criticism requires them to do so, when in fact literary criticism has for years now been moving more and more towards a method that examines this very aspect of literature. If children's book critics look for parity with their col-leagues outside the study of children's books, they must—if for no other more valuable reason—show how the concept of the implied reader relates to children as readers and to the books they read.

The idea of the implied reader derives from the understanding that it takes two to say a thing. In effect it suggests that in his book an author creates a relationship with a reader in order to discover the

35

meaning of the text. Wolfgang Iser, in *The Implied Reader*, puts it this way: he says that such a critical method 'is concerned primarily with the form of a work, insofar as one defines form basically as a means of communication or as a negotiation of insight' [p. 57].

To achieve this, an author, sometimes consciously sometimes not, creates, in Wayne C. Booth's words: 'an image of himself and another image of his reader; he makes his reader, as he makes his second self, and the most successful reading is one in which the created selves, author and reader, can find complete agreement.'[*The Rhetoric of Fiction*, p. 138]

The author's second self* is created by his use of various techniques: by the way, for example, he puts himself into the narrator—whether that be a third-person godlike all-seer or a first-person child character; by the way he comments on the events in the story; and by the attitude he adopts towards his characters and their actions, which he communicates in various ways, both subtle and obvious.

In the same way (and let me stress again, deliberately or otherwise) the reader's second self—the reader-in-the-book—is given certain attributes, a certain persona, created by techniques and devices which help form the narrative. And this persona is guided by the author towards the book's potential meanings.

Booth points out that a distinction must be made 'between myself as reader and the very often different self who goes about paying bills, repairing leaky faucets, and failing in generosity and wisdom. It is only as I read that I become the self whose beliefs must coincide with the author's. Regardless of my real beliefs and practices, I must subordinate my mind and heart to the book if I am to enjoy it to the full.' [p. 137]

3. The unyielding child reader

Booth expresses something mature literary readers have always understood: that a requirement of fulfilled readership is a willingness

---

*The term was revived by Kathleen Tillotson in her inaugural lecture at the University of London, published under the title 'The Tale and the Teller' (1959): 'Writing on George Eliot in 1877 Dowden said that the form that most persists in the mind after reading her novels is not any of the characters, but "one who, if not the real George Eliot, is that second self who writes her books, and lives and speaks through them." The "second self", he goes on, is "more substantial than any mere human personality" and has "fewer reserves"; while "behind it, lurks well pleased the veritable historical self secure from impertinent observation and criticism".' [p. 15] to give oneself up to the book. They have learned how to do this: how to lay aside their own prejudices and take on the prejudices of the text, how to enter into the book, becoming part of it while at the same time never abandoning their own being. In C. S. Lewis's words literature allowed him 'to become a thousand [people] and yet remain myself'.

Children, of course, have not completely learned how to do this; they have not discovered how to shift the gears of their personality according to the invitations offered by the book. In this respect they are unyielding readers. They want the book to suit them, tending to expect an author to take them as he finds them rather than they taking the book as they find it. One of the valuable possibilities offered by the critical method I look for is that it would make more intelligently understandable those books which take a child as he is but then draw him into the text; the books which help the child reader to negotiate meaning, help him develop the ability to receive a text as a literary reader does rather than making use of it for nonliterary purposes.

The concept of the implied reader and the critical method that follows from it help us to do just that. They help us establish the author's relationship with the (child) reader implied in the story, to see how he creates that relationship and to discover the meaning(s) he seeks to negotiate. Clearly, such understanding will lead us beyond a critical appreciation of the text towards that other essential activity of people concerned with children's books: how to mediate the books to their readers so that not only are individual books better appreciated by children but children are also helped to become literary readers.

II

We must examine one book closely in an attempt to reveal its implied reader. But before we come to that, it might be useful to consider some of the principal techniques by which an author can establish his tone—his relationship with his desired reader—and, of particular importance in children's books, by which he can draw the reader into the text in such a way that the reader accepts the role offered and enters into the demands of the book.

4. Style

Style is the term we use for the way a writer employs language to make his second self and his implied reader and to communicate his meaning. It is far too simplistic to suppose that this is just a matter of sentence structure and choice of vocabulary. It encompasses an author's use of image, his deliberate and unaware references, the assumptions he makes about what a reader will understand without explication or description, his attitude to beliefs, customs, characters in his narrative—all as revealed by the way he writes about them.

A simple example which allows a comparison between the style a writer employed when writing for adults and the alterations he made to it when rewriting the story for children, is provided by Roald Dahl. 'The Champion of the World' is a short story first published in *The New Yorker* and now included in *Kiss Kiss*. Some years afterwards Dahl rewrote the story for children under the title *Danny: The Champion of the World*. The original version could hardly be called difficult in subject or language. A ten-year-old of average reading ability could manage it without too much bother, should any child want to. Both versions are told in the first person; the adult narrator of the original is in some respects naïvely ingenuous, a device Dahl employs (following *New Yorker*-Thurber tradition) as a foil for the narrator's friend Claud, a worldly wise, unfazable character, and as a device to exaggerate into comic extravagance the otherwise only mildly amusing events of a fairly plain tale.

Because the original is written in this first-person, easily read narrative, which is naïve even in its emotional pitch, Dahl could transfer parts with minimal alterations straight from the original into the children's version. Yet even so, he made some interesting and significant changes. Here, for example, is the original description of the entry into the story of its arch-villain, Victor Hazel (differently spelt in the two tellings), whose unforgivable snobbery and unscrupulous selfishness are justification enough in the narrator's eyes to warrant poaching his pheasants:

> I wasn't sure about this, but I had a suspicion that it was none other than the famous Mr Victor Hazel himself, the owner of the land and the pheasants. Mr Hazel was a local brewer with an unbelievably arrogant manner. He was rich beyond words, and his property stretched for miles along either side of the valley. He was a self-made man with no charm at all and precious few virtues. He

loathed all persons of humble station, having once been one of them himself, and he strove desperately to mingle with what he believed were the right kind of folk. He rode to hounds and gave shooting-parties and wore fancy waistcoats, and every weekday he drove an enormous black Rolls-Royce past the filling-station on his way to the brewery. As he flashed by, we would sometimes catch a glimpse of the great glistening brewer's face above the wheel, pink as a ham, all soft and inflamed from drinking too much beer. [p. 209]

Here is the version recast for the children's telling:

I must pause here to tell you something about Mr Victor Hazell. He was a brewer of beer and he owned a huge brewery. He was rich beyond words, and his property stretched for miles along either side of the valley. All the land around us belonged to him, everything on both sides of the road, everything except the small patch of ground on which our filling-station stood. That patch belonged to my father. It was a little island in the middle of the vast ocean of Mr Hazell's estate.

Mr Victor Hazell was a roaring snob and he tried desperately to get in with what he believed were the right kind of people. He hunted with the hounds and gave shooting parties and wore fancy waistcoats. Every week-day he drove his enormous silver Rolls-Royce past our filling-station on his way to the brewery. As he flashed by we would sometimes catch a glimpse of the great glistening beery face above the wheel, pink as a ham, all soft and inflamed from drinking too much beer. [p. 49–50]

Dahl has simplified some of his sentences by chopping up the longer ones with full stops where commas are used in the adult version. And he does some cutting: he takes out the abstractions such as the comment about Hazel loathing people of humble station because he had once been one of them himself. Presumably Dahl felt children would not be able (or want) to cope either with the stylistic complexities of his first version or with the motivation ascribed to Hazel's behaviour. Whatever we may think about this, it certainly reveals Dahl's assumptions about his implied reader.

What he aims to achieve—and does—is a tone of voice which is clear, uncluttered, unobtrusive, not very demanding linguistically,

and which sets up a sense of intimate, yet adult-controlled, relationship between his second self and his implied child reader. It is a voice
often heard in children's books of the kind deliberately written for
them: it is the voice of speech rather than of interior monologue or
no-holds-barred private confession. It is, in fact, the tone of a
friendly adult storyteller who knows how to entertain children while
at the same time keeping them in their place. Even when speaking
outrageously about child-adult taboo subjects (theft by poaching in
Danny and, in this extract, harsh words about a grown-up), the tone
has a kind of drawing-room politeness. At its most typical it is a style
that speaks of 'the children' in the tale. Arthur Ransome marks a high
point in that traditional manner:

So the letters had been written and posted, and day after day the
children had been camping on the Peak of Darien by day, and
sleeping in the farmhouse by night. They had been out in the
rowing-boat with their mother, but they had always rowed the
other way so as not to spoil the voyage of discovery by going to the
island first. But with each day after the sending of the letters it had
somehow seemed less and less likely that there would ever be an
answer. The island had come to seem one of those places seen
from the train that belong to a life in which we shall never take part.
And now, suddenly, it was real. It was to be their island after all.
They were to be allowed to use the sailing-boat by themselves.
They were to be allowed to sail out from the little sheltered bay,
and round the point, and down the lake to the island. They were to
be allowed to land on the island, and to live there until it was time
to pack up again and go home to town and school and lessons. The
news was so good that it made them solemn. They ate their bread
and marmalade in silence. The prospect before them was too vast
for chatter. John was thinking of the sailing, wondering whether he
really remembered all that he had learnt last year. Susan was
thinking of the stores and the cooking. Titty was thinking of the
island itself, of coral, treasure, and footprints in the sand. Roger
was thinking of the fact that he was not to be left behind. He saw
for the first time that it was a good thing to be no longer the baby of
the family. Vicky was youngest now. Vicky would stay at home, and
Roger, one of the crew of a ship, was to sail away into the unknown
world. [pp. 16–17]

Ransome achieves precisely the same relationship with his reader as Dahl, and by pretty much the same stylistic qualities. Ransome's style is more fluid than Dahl's, gentler on the ear, better balanced and more tuneful. But it is essentially writing for children; no one, surely, can believe that, had Ransome been writing for adults—in the sense of an implied adult reader—he would have adopted the tone of voice so evident and so well created in *Swallows and Amazons*, from which the extract is taken.

Style can, as I say, work in a much more complex and subtly effective way than these two extracts suggest—or rather than my use of them here suggests. And we will look further into this aspect of the writer-reader relationship when we come to examine a major text.

5. Intermission: What the writers say . . .

Mention of Ransome calls to mind his famous much-quoted words about writing for children: 'You write not *for* children but for yourself, and if, by good fortune, children enjoy what you enjoy, why then you are a writer of children's books.'

All very well and, obviously, what Ransome believed about himself. But it is difficult to believe on the evidence of Ransome's books that, had he really thought he was speaking to an adult audience primarily, he would have adopted the same tone of voice or would have treated his stories in the ways he does. Even a traditional critical examination of his books, eschewing all thought of the reader, implied or otherwise (excepting of course the critic who never considers himself anything but an objective, and therefore somehow never a specific, reader—a matter Langman in the article already mentioned deals with very effectively), must surely reveal that Ransome's books are for children in quite specific ways, whatever Ransome himself said. Which is not to suggest that he, or any other writer who adopts this idea about himself as a writer, is dissembling. Rather, I want simply to reinforce Langman's observation: 'An author may write for a single person or a large public, for himself or for nobody. But the work itself implies the kind of reader to whom it is addressed and this may not coincide with the author's private view of his audience.'

Which proves one thing, if anything at all: we must be wary of using as evidence in criticism what an author says about himself, publicly or privately: a caution we have not sufficiently taken to heart in commenting on children's books. Over recent years there has been a fashion for calling the authors on stage to explicate themselves and their work in public and to defend it against the worst ravages of pedagogy and off-the-cuff criticism. That has been beneficial neither for the authors nor for their audiences.

6. Point of view

Tone of voice, style as a whole, very quickly establishes a relationship between author and reader; very quickly creates the image of the implied reader. In books where the implied reader is a child, authors tend to reinforce the relationship by adopting in their second self—giving the book, if you prefer—a very sharply focused point of view. They tend to achieve that focus by putting at the centre of the story a child through whose being everything is seen and felt.

This is more than simply a device. If literature for children is to have any meaning at all, it must primarily be concerned with the nature of childhood, not just the nature commonly shared by most children but the diversity of childhood nature too. For, like all literature, children's literature at its best attempts 'to explore, re-create and seek for meanings in human experience' (the phrase is Richard Hoggart's); this attempt is made with specific reference to children and their lives through the unique relationship between language and form.

But, at the level of creating the implied reader and of an author's need to draw a child reader into his book, this narrowing of focus by the adoption of a child point of view helps keep the author's second self—himself in the book—within the perceptual scope of his child reader. And the child, finding within the book an implied author whom he can befriend because he is of the tribe of childhood as well, is thus wooed into the book. He adopts the image of the implied child reader and is then willing, may even desire, to give himself up to the author and the book and be led through whatever experience is offered.

Thus the book's point of view not only acts as a means of creating the author-reader relationship but works powerfully as a solvent, melting away a child's non-literary approach to reading and re-forming him into the kind of reader the book demands.

Some authors, feeling constricted by a too narrowly child-focusing viewpoint, try to find ways of presenting a fuller picture of adulthood without losing the child-attracting quality of the narrower focus. A few have tried to do this directly, using adult characters and a point of view that shifts between a child-focus and an adult-focus, but very few of the few who have tried have succeeded. It remains one of the major problems for children's writers now. *Carrie's War* by Nina Bawden is well worth critical consideration as a very fine example of how an author creates an implied reader and of how adult characters can be revealed in much of their complexity without loss of definition for young readers.

Most writers approach the problem of adult-portrayal less directly. They tend to cast their tales in the form of fantasy, usually with animal-human characters. Robert C. O'Brien's *Mrs Frisby and the Rats of NIMH* provides a much enjoyed modern example; Kenneth Grahame's *The Wind in the Willows* probably the best known and most affectionately regarded; and Russell Hoban's *The Mouse and His Child* one of the most complexly layered and handled (for which reasons, no doubt, it is finding its most responsive audience not among children but among adolescents).

But if I wanted to select, in the context of my theme, two superlative examples that encompass a possible readership of about seven years old right on to adulthood, I would choose Alan Garner's *The Stone Book* to demonstrate the direct approach and Ted Hughes's *The Iron Man* as an example of the solution through fantasy.

7. Taking sides

It does not follow, of course, that a writer who places a child at the narrative centre of his tale necessarily or even intentionally forges an alliance with children. *Lord of the Flies* is entirely peopled by children, but no one would call it a book for children in any sense. (Adolescents enjoy it—or at least their teachers have decided they shall study it; but adolescents are not children, an understanding I have so far taken for granted.) Even the point of view of William Golding's book, though the narrative restricts itself to the child characters' points of view, is in fact profoundly adult in range and perceptions. And this is to say nothing about the style and the implied reader it helps create.

William Mayne, always published as a children's author but notoriously little read by children and much read by adults, may, for all I know, intend to be a writer for children. But what the tone of his books actually achieves, as Charles Sarland brilliantly uncovered in his article, 'Chorister Quartet', is an implied author who is an observer of children and the narrative: a watcher rather than an ally.

Even his dramatic technique seems deliberately designed to alienate the reader from the events and from the people described. This attitude to story is so little to be found in children's books that even children who have grown up as frequent and thoughtful readers find Mayne at his densest very difficult to negotiate. He wants his reader to stand back and examine what he, Mayne, offers in the same way that, as nearly as I can understand it, Brecht wanted his audiences to stand back from and contemplate the events enacted on stage.

As Sarland says, Mayne 'requires a degree of sophistication in the reader that would not normally be found in children of the same age as his characters. It is clear from the way he uses pace, dialogue, causal relationships, puns and wordplay that the last thing he wants is that the reader should be carried along on the tide of the narrative'. [p. 113]

There is, in other words, an ambivalence about Mayne's work that disturbs his relationship with his child reader. And this is made more unnerving by a fracture between a narrative point of view that seems to want to ally the book with children and narrative techniques that require the reader to disassociate from the story—to retreat and examine it dispassionately.

What Mayne may be trying to do—I say 'may be' because I am not sure that he *is* trying for it—is not impossible to achieve, though it is very difficult indeed to achieve for children. I have no space to delve into the matter here, fascinating though I find it, except to say as a pointer to those who want to follow this direction for themselves: Alan Garner's *The Stone Book*, besides the other extraordinary qualities it possesses, manages to balance these paradoxical demands, involving the reader with the narrative while at the same time helping him to stand back and contemplate it. And Garner makes it possible for children to participate like this at even quite an early time in their growth as readers, though the younger ones may require the mediation of an adult alongside them in order to enter into such a profound experience.

Taking sides can be crudely worked for, simply as a way of 'getting the child reader on your side'. Enid Blyton provides the obvious example. She quite literally places her second self on the side of the children in her stories and the readers she deliberately looks for. Her allegiance becomes collusion in a game of 'us kids against them adults'. Nothing reveals this more completely than her treatment of adult characters like the policeman Mr Goon in *The Mystery of the*

Strange Bundle. The unfortunate constable's name itself—chosen by the author, remember—indicates Blyton's attitude to the man, to his office, and her stance as one of the gang, one of the children in the story. Let's play this game together, she says openly and without embarrassment; let's have fun at the expense of the grown-ups; let's show them who's best; let's solve a mystery and have an adventure.

The very titles of her books reinforce this taking of sides. They act as an attraction to the book, raising in the reader expectations about the nature of the story to come that she never fails to satisfy. There are ten books in the *Mystery of* . . . series, eight in the Adventure series, and twelve 'about the Five Finder-Outers and Dog'.

Incident by incident Blyton sustains the collusion with her implied reader, sometimes letting him have the edge on the characters by telling him what they don't yet know, sometimes letting the characters have the edge on the reader by withholding details it later turns out the characters knew all the time. And adults get the edge only so that they can be done down later by the narrator, her characters and her readers.

There is about her stories a sense of secrets being told in whispers just out of earshot of the grown-ups, a subversive charm made all the more potent for being couched in a narrative style that sounds no more disturbing than the voice of a polite maiden aunt telling a bedtime story over cocoa and biscuits. Ultimately Blyton so allies herself with her desired readers that she fails them because she never takes them further than they are. She is a female Peter Pan, the kind of suffocating adult who prefers children never to grow up, because then she can enjoy their pretty foibles and dominate them by her adult superiority. This betrayal of childhood seeps through her stories: we see it as the underlying characteristic of her children who all really want to dominate each other as well as the adults.

Richmal Crompton is quite as canny; she too allies herself strongly with her child reader.* But her work has a redeeming quality—one among others: her ironic treatment of William, the Outlaws and their adventures. A skilled short-story writer, she structures her tales with an elegance outstanding in its craftsmanship and finish. But above all she brings to children's reading that essential element they must discover if they are to grow beyond the kind of writing Blyton's

*Of course, the William stories were first written for adults. But children soon adopted them, after which Richmal Crompton was never in doubt about her true audience.

epitomizes. For without an understanding of irony, literature—
beyond the merely plotful level—will never provide much pleasure
and certainly cannot yield up its deepest meanings.

Once an author has forged an alliance and a point of view that
engages a child, he can then manipulate that alliance as a device to
guide the reader towards the meanings he wishes to negotiate.
Wolfgang Iser provides a useful example, not from a specifically
children's book, where such a manoeuvre is too rarely used, but from
Oliver Twist. Iser cites the scene in which the hungry Oliver

> has the effrontery (as the narrator sees it) to ask for another plate of
> soup. In the presentation of this daring exploit, Oliver's inner
> feelings are deliberately excluded in order to give greater emphasis
> to the indignation of the authorities at such an unreasonable
> request. The narrator comes down heavily on the side of authority,
> and can thus be quite sure that his hard-hearted attitude will
> arouse a flood of sympathy in his readers for the poor starving
> child. [p. 116]

What such manipulation of the reader's expectations, allegiances,
and author-guided desires leads to is the further development of the
implied reader into an implicated reader: one so intellectually and
emotionally given to the book, not just its plot and characters but its
negotiation between author and reader of potential meanings, that
the reader is totally involved. The last thing he wants is to stop
reading; and what he wants above all is to milk the book dry of all it
has to offer, and to do so in the kind of way the author wishes. He
finally becomes a participant in the making of the book. He has
become aware of the 'tell-tale gaps'.

8. Tell-tale gaps

As a tale unfolds, the reader discovers its meaning. Authors can
strive, as some do, to make their meaning plain, leaving little room for
the reader to negotiate with them. Other authors leave gaps which the
reader must fill before the meaning can be complete. A skilful author
wishing to do this is somewhat like a play-leader: he structures his
narrative so as to direct it in a dramatic pattern that leads the reader
towards possible meaning(s); and he stage-manages the reader's
involvement by bringing into play various techniques which he knows
influence the reader's responses and expectations, in the way that

Iser, for example, described Dickens doing in *Oliver Twist* (7). Literature can be studied so as to uncover the gaps an author leaves for the reader to fill, these gaps taking two general forms.

The first is the more superficial. These gaps have to do with an author's assumptions, whether knowingly made or not, about his readers. Just as we saw in the Dahl extracts (4) how a writer's style revealed his assumptions about his implied reader's ability to cope with language and syntax, so we can also detect from a writer's references to a variety of things just what he assumes about his implied reader's beliefs, politics, social customs, and the like. Richmal Crompton in common with Enid Blyton, A. A. Milne, Edith Nesbit and many more children's authors assumed a reader who would not only be aware of housemaids and cooks, nannies and gardeners but would also be used to living in homes attended by such household servants. That assumption was as unconsciously made as the adoption of a tone of voice current among people who employed servants at the time the authors were writing.

These referential gaps, these assumptions of commonality, are relatively unimportant until they become so dominant in the text that people who do not—or do not wish to—make the same assumptions feel alienated by them as they read. This alienation, this feeling of repugnance, affects the child just as much as the adult, once the referential gaps become significant.

Far more important, however, is another form of tell-tale gap: these are the ones that challenge the reader to participate in making meaning. Making meaning is a vital concept in literary reading. Laurence Sterne refers to it directly in *Tristram Shandy*:

> No author, who understands the just boundaries of decorum and good breeding, would presume to think all: The truest respect which you can pay to the reader's understanding, is to halve this matter amicably, and leave him something to imagine, in his turn, as well as yourself.
>
> For my own part, I am eternally paying him compliments of this kind, and do all that lies in my power to keep his imagination as busy as my own. [p. 127]

Of course, it doesn't all depend on the author; he can deploy his narrative skills brilliantly, 'halving the matter amicably' with his reader. But unless a reader accepts the challenge, no relationship that seeks to discover meaning is possible. It is one of the responsibilities of children's writers, and a privileged one, so to write that children are led to understand how to read: how to accept the challenge.

Let me offer the crucial gap in Sendak's *Where the Wild Things Are* as example. In its pictorial as well as its textual art this masterpiece is compactly authored. One might be forgiven for supposing at first sight that there are no gaps of any kind for the reader to enter. But not so; there is one so vital that, unless the reader fills it, the profound meaning of the book cannot be discovered. It is the gap which demands that the reader supply the understanding that Max has dreamt his journey to the Wild Things, that in fact the Wild Things are Max's own creation. Once understood, that meaning having been made, the book opens itself to all sorts of other pleasurable discoveries which actually were clues to the meaning all along and which, once realized, present themselves as clues to yet further meaning. There is, for instance, in the first picture in the book, the Wild-Thingish doll hanging from a coathanger; and then, in the very next picture, there is the portrait of a Wild Thing framed and hung on the wall and signed 'by Max'.

Such guides to the reader may seem obvious to an adult, but children of four and five and six, who are the book's implied readers, make such a significant contribution and discover such details only if they give the book a willing attention of the same order as adults must give to filling the gaps in, say, Joyce's *Ulysses*.

Alan Garner's *The Stone Book* is built around three main images, each placed in precise relationship to each other so that they create two vital gaps which the reader must enter and fill before the potential meanings of the book become plain. Reiner Zimnik's *The Crane* is as halved as Sterne could wish; Zimnik's tone of voice is so sensible, so matter of fact, so gentle and everyday, you can suppose the meaning(s) of his story must be so too. But in fact the book is heavy with possibilities and is not at all easy to plumb intellectually, though emotionally—as an increasing number of teachers are finding after introducing it to their nine- to twelve-year-olds—it is powerfully attractive.

9. In sum . . .

. . . and before we begin an exploration of one text.

I am suggesting that the concept of the implied reader, far from unattended to by literary critics in Europe and America, offers us a critical approach which concerns itself less with the subjects portrayed in a book than with the means of communication by which the reader is brought into contact with the reality presented by an author. It is a method which could help us determine whether a book is for children or not, what kind of book it is, and what kind of reader (or, to put it another way, what kind of reading) it demands. Knowing this will help us to understand better how to teach not just a particular book but particular books to particular children.

I have been trying to sketch in some of the more significant ways in which specific responses are provoked in a reader, the techniques that make up what Kenneth Burke in *The Philosophy of Literary Form* has called 'the strategy of communication'. This is achieved by major techniques such as I have described and by a variety of other devices such as what an author discloses to his reader and what he conceals, the way he signals his intentions, his evocation of suspense, the introduction of the unexpected, and the way he can play about with the reader's expected responses to the narrative.

All these create a relationship between author and reader, which I have used the word 'tone' to denote; and an author, consciously or otherwise, reveals in his narrative, through the way he uses all these techniques and by other signals too, what he wants from his reader, what kind of relationship he looks for.

Now I want to examine some of these matters at work in one book, Lucy Boston's *The Children of Green Knowe*.

III

10. Why *The Children of Green Knowe?*

For three reasons:

Mrs Boston is a much admired and respected writer; her first children's book lends itself to my critical needs here.

Not only is she much respected, but she is historically important. *The Children of Green Knowe* appeared in 1954 and was one of the first of the new wave of children's books that marks the outcropping since the Second World War. I think it intelligently arguable that this book directly influenced a number of the writers who began work in the 50s and 60s. (Philippa Pearce's *Tom's Midnight Garden*, Alan Garner's *The Weirdstone of Brisingamen* and the work of

William Mayne owe a considerable debt to Lucy Boston. Discuss.)

Mrs Boston has said publicly some interesting things about her work, which provide an example of the kind of authorial self-comment I warned against earlier. During a talk given in November 1968 to the Children's Book Circle (a gathering of children's book editors in London who meet to discuss their professional concerns) Mrs Boston said:

> Is there a conscious difference in the way I write for grown-ups and children? No, there is no difference of approach, style, vocabulary or standard. I could pick out passages from any of the books and you would not be able to tell what age it was aimed at. [p. 36]

Let's see. The opening of *Yew Hall*, Lucy Boston's first book, and written for adults (or, to use her word, grown-ups):

> Possibly it was their voices that made me decide that I could share my house with them, so that after having once refused, I repented and told them that they could come. He was a huge man, handsome like a statue in St Paul's. His martial features and great neck suggested at once to the imagination the folds of a marble cloak drawn back across a superlative torso and looped over an arm to free the incredible giant legs in their marble tights. He was so near to the type classified as admirable at the turn of the eighteenth century that his own personality might have escaped my notice if it had not been that his voice was as soft and warm in quality as a man's voice could possibly be. There was nothing feminine about it. It was like a breeze in the tops of a forest, and he gave the impression, that afterwards was amply confirmed, of having so much space to live in that he need never knock elbows with or trip over anyone else. Well might he be self-satisfied—like America he had no need of imports. A general comfort radiated from his bigness—a big heart, a big fire, a big meal, a big bed, a big pair of shoes; and, I suppose, we must also think of a big stick, a big clap of thunder. [pp. 9–10]

Compare the opening passage of her first children's book, published the same year (see extract below): there are unmistakable differences in approach, style and vocabulary. The urbanity of *Yew Hall* establishes very quickly a tone that implies a literate, adult reader. The handsome statues of St Paul's, the martial features and superlative torso, the type classified as admirable at the turn of the eighteenth century, America having no need of imports: this one paragraph is littered with references that expect a reader who can match the author's cultural and social background: the educated English middle class. The writing is confident, witty, slightly superior ('Possibly it was their voices that made me decide that I could share my house with them . . .'), the kind of writing one would not be ashamed to be caught reading by one's butler.

What of *The Children of Green Knowe*? Who is its implied reader? Let's look at it under the headings suggested in II.

11. Style

Here are the opening paragraphs of *The Children of Green Knowe*:

A little boy was sitting in the corner of a railway carriage looking out at the rain, which was splashing against the windows and blotching downward in an ugly, dirty way. He was not the only person in the carriage, but the others were strangers to him. He was alone as usual. There were two women opposite him, a fat one and a thin one, and they talked without stopping, smacking their lips in between sentences and seeming to enjoy what they said as much as if it were something to eat. They were knitting all the time, and whenever the train stopped the click-clack of their needles was loud and clear like two clocks. It was a stopping train—more stop than go—and it had been crawling along through flat flooded country for a long time. Everywhere there was water—not sea or rivers or lakes, but just senseless flood water with the rain splashing into it. Sometimes the railway lines were covered by it, and then the train-noise was quite different, softer than a boat.

'I wish it was *the* Flood', thought the boy, 'and that I was going to the Ark. That would be fun! Like the circus. Perhaps Noah had a whip and made all the animals go round and round for exercise. What a noise there would be, with the lions roaring, elephants trumpeting, pigs squealing, donkeys braying, horses whinnying, bulls bellowing, and cocks and hens always thinking they were going to be trodden on but unable to fly up to the roof where all the other birds were singing, screaming, twittering, squawking and cooing. What must it have sounded like, coming along on the tide? And did Mrs Noah just knit, knit and take no notice?'

The two women opposite him were getting ready for the next station. They packed up their knitting and collected their parcels and then sat staring at the little boy. He had a thin face and very large eyes; he looked patient and rather sad. They seemed to notice him for the first time. [pp. 9–10]

The language in *Yew Hall* tends towards the Latinate. *Green Knowe* is much more firmly Anglo-Saxon. Rain is splashing and blotching, lips are smacking, knitting needles click-clack, not to mention Tolly's own list of participial verbs describing Noah's animals. This makes for a style not only simpler to read but far more active than a Latinate one, far more concrete in an everyday and child-appealing sense.

There is, however, as Mrs Boston claims, no lowering of standard between the two books. *Green Knowe* is just as densely and richly textured—perhaps is even more richly textured—than *Yew Hall*. But the images and the words used to communicate them are quite different in the experiential demands made on the reader. At the crudest level *Yew Hall* requires familiarity wth St Paul's Cathedral, the late eighteenth century and the economy of the United States if one is to enjoy all Mrs Boston has to offer. *Green Knowe* requires no such sophistication. You need only to have seen some rain, have been on a train, know something about the story of Noah and the Flood, and to have observed women knitting for the text to be completely open to you. After that you need only put at Mrs Boston's disposal a sympathetic imagination and she leads you off in a very clearly signposted direction. Even from these three opening paragraphs we can see she is busy with sensual experience: the sight, sound, feel, and sense of things. It is a direction in which her story will take young readers a very long way.

For sure, then, the style of *The Children of Green Knowe* is much more accessible to a child reader, and comparison with the style of *Yew Hall*, which seems so much more confidently natural to Mrs Boston—one feels it is closer to her own thinking voice—leads one to suppose its implied reader is a child. At the very least the style appeals to the child-in-the-adult, possessing that very tone of voice I earlier suggested is traditionally the English tone used in telling stories to children: direct, clear, polite, firm, uncluttered. And Mrs Boston achieves it admirably.

We must discover whether or not the other aspects of her book reinforce the impression given by her style.

Tolly is seven; remarkable for his age, a child of a very particular class. His father and stepmother are in Burma; the boy has been put into boarding school, left for the holidays with the headmistress and her old father, and then sent alone on a train journey to visit his great-grandmother, Mrs Oldknow, who lives in a large old house. Throughout, the story is told from Tolly's point of view. Only occasionally is there a brief shift for some narrative purpose, as when the two women in the train 'sat staring at the little boy. He had a thin face and very large eyes; he looked patient and rather sad. They seemed to notice him for the first time.' Otherwise, the perceptions are all the boy's.

Even Mrs Oldknow, so central a character in the story, is seen only from the outside. Her private thoughts and perceptions remain enigmatic, and influentially so: she occupies a somewhat mysteriously attractive place in the book. One wonders about her, and feels too a little daunted by her, a little afraid of her secret knowingness. The reader gets that impression from a subtly handled feature of the book. All along one cannot help feeling that it is Mrs Oldknow who is telling the story. And probably the feeling would not be so strong were it not for the stories Mrs Oldknow tells Tolly at night. They are about the children who lived in the house and died in the Plague of 1665. But then, the rest of the book is also about a boy in the house. Isn't the whole book therefore a story by Mrs Oldknow? Has she, in fact, invented Tolly? Or isn't she, at the very least, telling his story, and doing it so well because she *knows*—can see into children's minds, as children so often believe some adults can, and tell what is going on in them?

So, though the story is told from Tolly's point of view—apart, of course, from Mrs Oldknow's stories about the other, long-ago children—Mrs Oldknow herself seems in control of it. These two things together stimulate a strong sense of alliance among Mrs Oldknow, Tolly and the reader, thus placing the author unmistakably on the reader's side.

13. Taking sides

Before the story has gone far enough to establish the strong relationship I've just described, Mrs Boston is signalling her allegiance. The opening paragraphs of the book reveal her sympathetic understanding of a small boy's response to the world about him, and in particular the world as it surrounds Tolly at that moment on the train. Every slight detail serves this end, from the clacking needles and the train being more stop than go, to the child-accurate observation of the rain and the flood and the train noise.

Then the two women take notice, and their conversation with Tolly sets him thinking about his circumstances. Now Mrs Boston reveals unequivocally whose side she is on: Tolly being miserably shy of his headmistress, the kind Miss Spudd, who yet always calls him 'dear'.

When Tolly at last meets his great-grandmother, wondering if she is a witch and whether he will be afraid of her (the terrible business of meeting strange relatives), Mrs Boston-Oldknow (for Mrs Boston's second self must surely be Mrs Oldknow) declares her allegiance openly: 'What does one generation more or less matter? I'm glad you have come. It will seem lovely to me. How many years of you have I wasted?' A declaration of friendship, if not of love, which is reinforced by a further shift from adult-child allegiance to collusion no more than a page later:

At that moment the fire went *pop!* and shot a piece of wood out into the room. *Pop!* again.
'Buttons! Who said buttons? Poor Mrs Noah.' Tolly chased the sparks and trod on them to put them out.
'Why do you live in a castle?' he said, looking round.
'Why not? Castles were meant to live in.'
'I thought that was only in fairy tales. Is it a real castle?'
'Of course.'
'I mean, do things happen in it, like the castles in books?'
'Oh yes, things happen in it.'
'What sort of things?'
'Wait and see! I'm waiting too, to see what happens now that you are here. Something will, I'm sure.' [p. 20]

Something is being proposed here: at the least a game, at the most something more mysteriously magical, and it is to be an adventure enacted between Tolly and Mrs Oldknow.

Next morning, the adventure begins: it involves Tolly's long-ago child relatives—whether as ghosts or not we hope to discover— household toys, garden animals, and Mrs Oldknow. Being cut off by the flood simply asserts actually and symbolically the private collusive world inhabited by the boy and the old woman.

But the collusion is not just a means of disposing the reader to the book: its profoundest meaning depends upon the nature of the relationship.

14. Tell-tale gaps

Game or ghost story? More than a game and not just a ghost story. Each time we think that at last Tolly is indisputably seeing apparitions of Toby, Alexander and Linnet, Mrs Boston withdraws confirmation.

A crucial scene comes after the snowfall. A tree's branches form a cave, which Tolly enters and there seems to meet and hear speaking the three ghosts; Alexander even plays his flute. But the scene ends: 'Had he been dreaming?' And when Tolly creeps out of his snow-cave, 'Somewhere in the garden a thrush was trying to whistle Alexander's tune.' We are left wondering still.

Later Mrs Oldknow leaves Tolly alone in the house, and Boggis too is gone. Surely now the ghosts will emerge and they, Tolly and the reader can meet undeniably. But no. Despite the house being empty of others and dark coming on, so that the stage is set for a final exciting ghost-drama, our expectations raised for a climax (how many other writers have prepared us so before), Mrs Boston will not satisfy us: 'For some reason [Tolly] felt convinced that until his great-grandmother returned, not so much as a marble would move in the house.' She has employed a device similar to Dickens's in *Oliver Twist*: reader's expectations raised, and deliberately dashed. We are forced to wonder why.

Here is the amicable halving of this book; here is a tell-tale gap which the reader must enter if the book's true meaning is to be negotiated. Whatever is going on in the story can only be enacted between Mrs Oldknow and Tolly. Nothing happens when they are apart. Together, their lives have followed a pattern. During the day, Tolly explores and plays, sometimes on his own, sometimes with Mrs Oldknow, sometimes with Boggis, but always, however gently and subtly suggested, at the instigation of his great-grandmother. She, like a superlatively wise play-leader, offers opportunities for Tolly to enjoy himself through experiences that enliven the world to him. He is led to look closely, hear clearly, touch sensitively, think imaginatively. The book is laden with instances in which Tolly encounters objects and, by sensing them and playing with them, imaginatively perceives the life in them.

These moments extend from the purely sensational—

> In the fire the snow drifting down the chimney was making the only noise it ever can—a sound like the striking of fairy matches; though sometimes when the wind blows you can hear the snow like a gloved hand laid against the window. [p. 64]

—to lengthy passages in which Tolly's exploration of a room or a part of the garden or of a toybox is described in close and carefully imaged detail. The walk through the snow that leads to the snow-cave scene is one such.

Punctuating these descriptions of the day-to-day activities are four stories told by Mrs Oldknow to Tolly at bedtime. This device suits the apparently naturalistic plot: Tolly is on holiday with his great-grandmother; the house and gardens provide his daily adventures; before bed he is given his fictional adventure. But these four stories are not just any stories: they are about the three long-ago children and their horse Feste, one story for each. Some critics—John Rowe Townsend in *A Sense of Story*, for instance—have felt this an awkward construction. To my mind it is not only a pattern that creates a satisfying rhythm in the book—entirely suited, as I say, to the plot's boy-on-holiday structure—but it actually makes the book's true meaning possible.

We are led to see things this way: Tolly and Mrs Oldknow fantasize about Toby and Alexander and Linnet. Tolly may or may not actually see their ghosts, and enjoys the game. But the three long-ago children have undeniable reality only in the stories Mrs Oldknow tells about them. There they live in their own right, not as spectres raised by Tolly and his great-grandmother, just as Tolly and Mrs Oldknow have a reality in their own right only as characters in Mrs Boston's story about them. Stories, Mrs Boston is telling us, are the means by which we give life to ourselves and the objects around us. Stories, in fact, create meaning.

Strangely enough, in the very talk to the Children's Book Circle in which she claimed no difference between her writing for adults and her writing for children, Mrs Boston also said:

> My approach has always been to explore reality as it appears, and

from within to see how far imagination can properly expand it. Reality, after all, has no outside edge. I never start with a fantasy and look for a peg to hang it on. As far as I deliberately try to do anything other than to write a book that pleases me, I would like to remind adults of joy, now considered obsolete—and would like to encourage children to use and trust their senses for themselves at first hand—their ears, eyes and noses, their fingers and the soles of their feet, their skins and their breathing, their muscular joy and rhythms and heartbeats, their instinctive loves and pity and their awe of the unknown. This, not the telly, is the primary material of thought. It is from direct sense stimulus that imagination is born ... [p. 36]

Nowhere has an author so exactly stated her aims, and in few books has an author achieved her highest aims so certainly as Mrs Boston does in *The Children of Green Knowe*. Through Tolly, guided by Mrs Boston's second self, her implied reader is brought to grips with the direct sense stimulus that gives birth to life-expanding imagination. By any standard this is a fine achievement, all the more remarkable for its simplicity.

15. Lucy Boston's implied reader

Mrs Boston makes no impossible demands on her child reader's ability to construct meaning from words. Her style is approachable, uncomplicated, specific rather than abstract. The first Green Knowe book is not long; its episodic and day-by-day rhythm punctuated by the stories-within-the-story makes it easy to read in unexhausting parts. Her alliance with her young reader is persuasive. The now almost old-fashioned middle-classness of Tolly's and Mrs Oldknow's life (and Mrs Boston's preference for it) is strong but not so dominantly obtrusive as to be a disadvantage. (The polite formality of the collusion between Mrs Oldknow and Tolly is nowadays amusing. Even though they are playing a game, Tolly must always behave impeccably; he commits only one naughty act throughout the whole book: he writes on the newly whitewashed wall in Boggis's room, a wickedness allowed to pass without censure, of course, because it is done in a servant's room, not in the main house. Even Boggis, old retainer, wants to preserve the benevolent hierarchical social tradition, to the point of tolerating his daughter's indiscretion because it provides him with a male heir to his post. The book is deeply conservative and traditionalist; a political attitude which disposes children all the more readily to the story, for most children prefer things to remain as they always have been.)

All Mrs Boston requires of her reader is a willingness to enter into the spirit of sensuous discovery. Given this, she deploys her craft very subtly indeed towards her stated aims. And that she is speaking primarily to children I have no doubt.

The Child's
Changing Story

The theme of the 18th Congress of the International Board on Books for Young People, held at Churchill College, Cambridge, 6–10 September 1982, was 'Story in the Child's Changing World'. When one of the main speakers, Bruno Bettelheim, was prevented by illness from coming to Cambridge to deliver his paper, I was invited to speak in his place. The following text is reprinted from *Signal* 40, January 1983.

*

In every language, in every part of the world, Story is the fundamental grammar of all thought and communication.

By telling ourselves *what happened, to whom, and why* we not only discover ourselves and the world, but we change and create ourselves and the world too.

Unquestionably, the world we live in—the people-made world— is changing, as is our understanding of the universe our world inhabits.

If this is true, and if Story reflects, captures, finds meanings, even creates meanings, in relation to the world we live in, then Story must be changing—or should be, or ought to be changing—in tune with what our world is and is becoming.

At this point, let us remind ourselves that Story is not just about the *who* and the *what* and the *why*. It is not only about character, action, and motivation. Not just about Content. It is quite as importantly about the *how*. About Form. As our finest critical readers have so often shown, how a story is made tells us quite as much about the world as a writer understands it as anything in a story's content.

In the days when people still truly believed that the world worked according to an unalterable law of linear and sequential process, a neat and tidy matter of one identifiable cause leading to an identifiable result, they made stories work like that too. Think of the magnificent novels of Jane Austen, for example, or of Dostoevsky's *Crime and Punishment*. The plots in that kind of writing might adequately be described as being made of one damn thing after another.

There are of course writers who still tell stories that way. Most writers do, in fact, whether for children or not. But to more and more of us they seem naïve and unreal. They do not match up to the world as we find it. Perhaps a lot of people who might read literature do not do so because they think this too.

In what ways, then, is Story changing? And what have the changes to do with children? The answers to these questions may be found by playing a quite simple game. The game begins by writing down what you consider to be the greatest changes that have come about in the twentieth century: the ones that affect our lives most and may continue to do so for many years ahead.

You will not be surprised to learn that I have already played this part of the game, and that now you must prepare yourselves to be charmed by the results. Many changes come readily to mind. For now the five that seem to me most important are all we have time for.

I

At the top of my list comes The General Theory of Relativity. I will not insult your intelligence by pretending that I either fully understand or could adequately explain this extraordinary system of thought. But it is surely hard to dissent from the conclusion taught about it to children by that excellent compilation, *The World Book Encyclopedia*. 'Relativity', it states, 'has changed the whole philosophical and physical notions of space and time'.

You may recall that when an old lady pleaded with Einstein to explain the theory simply the great man is said to have replied, 'Madam, when you are sitting on a sofa with your boyfriend, two hours seem like two seconds. When you are sitting on a red hot stove, two seconds seem like two hours.'

Relativity has changed our ideas about time, space, cause and effect. That old definition of Story, *what happens to whom and why*, is having to change in order to accommodate extra elements into the formula: the elements *where*, *when*, and *seen by whom*? Relativity requires that we look at everything from more than one point of view.

Of course, stories have always taken place somewhere and at some supposed time and have had to be recounted by someone. But these were considered subordinate elements to the matter of character, action and motive. Now we know that character, action and motive are each and together fundamentally involved with when and where they are, and when and where the events take place. We also know that an infinite number of influences lie beyond the local and immediate context—beyond, if you like, the story itself—and may also have a part in the story. In other words no story can ever have a finite beginning or a finite end. No story can ever be a closed system, nor is the story ever of only one maker, one author.

There is always more than one storymaker, not just because every human author is subject to all kinds of exterior legacies but because every story of any kind whatever, by the very nature of Story, is told by more than one storyteller.

There is, to start with, the writer him or herself, a human being who lives a life of a complexity that extends beyond the limits of any story to contain.

Then, in making a story, the storyteller selects what to tell from all the possibilities available, decides how to combine the selections— how to tell them—and thus constructs not just a particular tale but also the persona of a narrator. We are grateful to various kinds of critic for showing us this aspect of storymaking: phenomenologists, structuralists, narratologists.

Now we come to the person who receives the story: the reader. He must 'take the story over', must reinvent it within himself. No reader can read passively. No reader can help but reshape a tale as he makes it his own. We know this to be true from our everyday experience. We know, for example, that every time we talk to each other about a story we discover that everyone emphasizes in slightly different ways this or that part, notices this or that detail, reacts differently to this or that element, and so on, making each reading one of a variety of subtly different understandings. Every group of readers gives every story many different shapes based on an original pattern. And the same thing happens within ourselves. Our sense of what a story is changes even as we talk and think about it, and every time we reread it.

At the very least, then, there are three storytellers involved in the making of every story. Knowing this, we cannot evade it either as authors or as readers. That knowledge has itself become part of what Story is and can be.

Similarly, there are numerous time-event relationships involved in every story. Briefly, there is the time it takes us to read the writing that communicates the tale. There is the time scale of the secondary world of the story itself, whether that happens within a few consecutive hours, as in *The Shrinking of Treehorn*, or over a period of many years, as in *Robinson Crusoe*. And there is the time that every story goes on living (and changing) in our memories, as my memory of Aesop's *Fables* has kept them alive for me for more than forty years.

Far more subtly interesting time scales than these occupy the space in stories, for Relativity has shown us that time need not be regarded as constant, except in the crude matter of clock time, by which we agree to regulate our workaday lives. We are now in possession of images that help us to think of time—and to use it—as T. S. Eliot did in one of the great poems about Relativity, *Four Quartets*. In 'Burnt Norton' Eliot gave us the now familiar lines:

> Time present and time past
> Are both perhaps present in time future
> And time future contained in time past.

And then, summing it up as the starting point of 'East Coker': 'In my beginning is my end.'

We can see some of this put simply to work for young readers in a short novel still regrettably unattended to in my own country but well regarded, I know, in its country of origin, the United States, and, I think, in France too. In *Slake's Limbo* Felice Holman tells the story of thirteen-year-old Slake's life underground in the New York subway, where he has taken refuge from the bully-boys who oppress him on the streets. This is managed sequentially, with some flashbacks at the beginning to explain Slake's present circumstances. But interleaved, so to speak, with the story of Slake's 121 days alone is the story of Willis Joe, driver of a subway train and eventually, when the two stories cross tracks, rescuer of Slake. Willis Joe's story ranges across his life: back to what it has been, forward to what he wishes it could be.

So here we have the time scale of Slake's 121 days set against the scale of Willis Joe's life; and while Willis Joe travels through time as well as through the subway tunnels, Slake travels nowhere much: he lives wholly in the present. Both characters are watched and reported to us by a narrator who adopts different attitudes to each: standing closer to Willis Joe than to the book's primary protagonist, but fascinated by the minutiae of Slake's Crusoe-like existence.

Time and space shift within this novel in ways that add significant meanings as well as density of thought to what would have been a much less striking and pertinent book, had the author told her tale only in the old way.

What is it then that Relativity activates in Story? These things at least: multiple narrators; simultaneity of different points of view; multipresentness of time; a place inside the story for the reader to be and to take part; an open system into and out of the story.

II

Second on my list of Big Changes is the word Space. Meaning the space that our planet inhabits, the universe itself. The blast-off from Earth, our exit into space, the setting down of a man on the moon, the brilliantly successful and useful manned and unmanned flights being conducted in the direction of the stars: these were made possible by Einstein's Theory and have caused a change in our view of what we are, and of the place where we live, and of our present and future.

To me one of the most deeply moving, most poignant, most revolutionary images I have ever seen was that first picture of the orb of Earth photographed by a man in space. As soon as I saw it, there came strongly back to my mind another image which produced in me exactly similar reactions.

When I was three I was taken by my mother to the house of my over-eighty-year-old great-grandmother. I do not think I had ever seen her before, and now she was dead. I remember standing on the floor surrounded by the feet and legs of aunts and uncles and grandparents, and from my lowly vantage gazing up at the underneath of a huge wooden box which seemed to me like a strange-shaped sideboard supported on stilts. Then an aunt picked me up and held me high over the box so that I could look down into the face of the dead woman lying inside, her head resting on a shiny white pillow trimmed with lace, her body so flatly covered by a stark white gown trimmed with pink that the waxen, taut-skinned face, with its closed and sunken eyes, looked to me as though it was all there was of her.

There and then, that startling vision of age and death changed my infant attitude to life. I could not have said what that change meant, but I knew it had happened, and now, forty-five years later, I could begin to explain. Great changes happen like that, and we may take many years to tell ourselves what they mean. It is part of an author's work to help us absorb such changes and understand them; indeed, that is what we are talking about when we use the phrase 'the artist's responsibility'.

I am not alone, I think, in finding the sight of Earth hanging in space so affecting. Our exit into the universe has caused a shift in our perspective, has forced on us a re-evaluation of what we are and what we can be. Most importantly it has given humanity a new sense of an ending.

Every author knows the importance of *direction* in storytelling: of knowing where you are going. Direction itself is determined not necessarily by knowing the precise details of an ending, but of having a sense of it. However, every story has two endings. There is the acknowledged end, which is the conclusion of that particular tale, as Max wakes after his encounter with the Wild Things to find his supper waiting and still hot, or as Charlotte dies after rescuing Wilbur and leaves behind her newborn children to carry on spinning—though to Wilbur they can never be what Charlotte was: a true friend and a great writer.

The second ending is the unacknowledged ending. This comes from—gets its direction from—the particularities of the story itself interacting with the author's view of life and of the society in which he lives. Thus in *Where the Wild Things Are* the unacknowledged ending is directed by a belief that through a proper valuing of, and attention to, our inner story life (our day and night dreaming, if you like) people can come into a healthful—a happy—relationship with their individual, inner lives and with one another. All Sendak's work is controlled by that sense of an ending, which envisions an idyllic, healed, and integrated state of being.

No one can write stories without taking into account the expansion of our lives away from Earth and into space. Away from the limited, cramped, minutely insignificant world in which we live, into a universe we know more clearly every day to be ever bigger, ever more astonishing, ever more fascinating than we could have imagined. We are, we now know, living on a microscopically small speck of dust lost on a vast seashore. We know we are not the lords of creation, not the centre of all life. We know our speck of dust is becoming uncomfortably crowded, a place which in any case by the natural course of things some of us are ready to leave, as all growing up, healthy children like to leave home. We could, of course, lock the doors, bar the windows, and shut ourselves in. The sense of an ending you would get from any story that proposed such a course (and there are plenty of them) would be quite different from the sense of an ending you would get in a story directed by the proposition that the doors should be thrown wide open and that we should be encouraged to explore the countryside beyond the garden gate.

Two kinds of ending. And two kinds of space: outer-space—the exterior universe of our habitation; and inner-space—the interior universe of our personalities, of our conscious and unconscious beings. Just as we have taken our first steps into the outer outer-space, so we have expanded the frontiers of conscious exploration of our inner-space. Relativity applies to both: and Freud and Jung have revised our ideas and knowledge about inner-space in just as startling a fashion as Einstein and the astrophysicists have about outer-space. Fascinatingly, both kinds of explorer report to us very similar adventures: the spaces seem remarkably alike.

Sendak's explorations use Story, adapted to modern notions, to go into inner-space. So too, we now realize, do the old folk-fairy tales, though there are still people who try to naturalize them as crude forms of social realism, banal tales about justice, hope, and tolerance. Our absent speaker, Bruno Bettelheim, would no doubt have helped us here.

E. B. White's *Charlotte's Web*, however, is about our exterior world, and is controlled by the Judaeo-Christian sense of an ending, in which continuity towards a possible—again to put it crudely—'happy' end is achieved by individual acts of sacrifice carried out in the consequential historic line, one generation to another, like runners in a relay race: good, let's say, running against evil, each runner handing on the baton of a good, or an evil, life to the next. Death, in this kind of story, relates all life to some other plane, some other sphere of being, and is not discussed except as a fact of individual experience. It is used as the closing of a door, an end in itself, which by implication requires a beginning of equal character in

65

the birth of a new person as one of the sacrificial acts of the old. The story and the storyteller remain earthbound in every sense.

In brief: Our first exit into space was a narrative event which focused into a dramatic image our revised understandings about the nature and extent of our inner and outer universes, and gave us a revised sense of an ending. Relativity, and other changes we shall come to in a moment, gave us some understanding of how to deal with the inexhaustible complexities we now recognize. In order to remain vital as the grammar of our thought, as the means by which all of us—scientists or not, clever or not, rich and poor, child and adult—think about ourselves, Story, and therefore storytellers, have to take all this into conscious account.

Which means that Story has to change. The core of the change is outlined by Hayden White in a recent issue of *Critical Inquiry*, where he asks the question: 'Does the world really present itself to perception in the form of well-made stories, with central subjects, proper beginnings, middles, and ends, and a coherence that permits us to see "the end" in every beginning?' [p. 27] To which I find myself forced to give the answer, 'No, not any more it doesn't.' Some authors, giving that same answer, have tried to find ways of representing the apparent absence of coherence. For my part, I have to say that it seems more important to me, especially in writing for young people, not to submit to incoherence but to search out new patterns of coherence and ways of making stories that represent those new patterns. This indeed is the narrative problem of our time. If we ignore it and retreat into the old ways, or simply suffocate in incoherence, then Story will fail us and our literature will become one long suicide note.

Of course, while there are people left who care about the survival of the human race, this won't happen. Story *is* changing, new patterns *are* being found, even in children's books.

A few small examples. In *Come Away from the Water, Shirley* John Burningham expresses in a story the interaction of inner- and outer-space so that quite young children can become aware of what is an everyday part of their experience. Sendak, as usual, does everything at once. *Outside Over There*—which my wife, Nancy, not without ironic pertinence, insists on calling *Inside Under Here*—tells a story of inner-space in images of outer-space and brings to bear on it the relativities of narrative. Look, for instance, at the story going on in the picture windows behind Ida while she hugs the changeling and murmurs 'How I love you', then dashes the ice thing to the floor, expostulates, and puts on her mama's yellow rain cloak; and think what those combined images might mean in relation to time, space and narrative purpose. Consider the time-space and narrative complexities of Mozart in his summerhouse by the stream as Ida carries the baby back home. Most curious of all, consider the alsatian dog, especially as drawn in the last doublespread. I can imagine some critics telling us that the dog is the hermeneutic problem of the book. We could go on much longer, for *Outside Over There* is a marvellously rich example of an author solving contemporary problems of Story.

Anthony Browne, in his treatment of *Hansel and Gretel*, shows how an old tale that offers itself to contemporary Story understandings can integrate with newly self-conscious narrative techniques—the old tradition living still; because it in any case belongs to the deep exploration of inner-space. See how he places representations of external, concrete objects—trees, a cat, triangularity of shapes like half-drawn curtains, shadows, pictures on walls—together so as to generate meanings that refer to inner-space realities: emotions, neuroses, abstract ideas. Look too at the way he uses pictures and words on every doublespread, part of which is a small image, a close-up if you like, of a detail that is not included in the main picture opposite, nor mentioned in the words, but that increases the density of meaning and adds a time-space shift to the whole.

These are all picture books. I use them here as examples because I can hope we will all have seen them; they cross our language barriers more easily than novels. But I could with more time refer in the same way to stories like Alan Garner's *Red Shift* and Robert Cormier's *I Am the Cheese* to show similar effects and to show how Relativity and our exit into space have affected them.

III

Mention of Anthony Browne helps me make a transition between the second and third words on my list of Big Changes, for *Hansel and Gretel*, like an earlier book of his, *A Walk in the Park*, is, at least in part, about Gender. And Gender is my third word.

I once asked a group of a hundred or so very tough inner-city fourteen-year-olds to jot down in order of preference the subjects about which they would most like to read stories. Two subjects were far and away the most popular. The first was sex and the second was violence. Their choice is supported by the highest authority. In the Old Testament of the Judaeo-Christian Bible, in the fourth chapter of the First Book of Genesis, after God has created the world and then Adam and Eve, the first story—the first story about people, that is—is about Adam knowing Eve, and the second is about their son Cain killing their son Abel. I expect there is an academic dissertation somewhere showing that numerically most of the stories in the world are about the relations between men and women, and that most of that majority are about the violence men and women do to each other during the experience we call love.

Truly, there is nothing new about Story and The Sexes. But I most carefully avoided using the word Sex in my list of Big Changes. What has come about in our century is a changed understanding—at least in Western society—of masculinity and femininity. We now recognize that each of the sexes combines both genders, the change being that now it really matters. Our future depends on getting it right. And we have changed our attitudes to what the 'rightness' means. The urge to a final, fruitful (the word can only be) marriage between the two elements in everyone's nature is being forced on us by our revised sense of an ending and has become one of the great modern imperatives.

I am not suggesting that the goal is a kind of undistinguishable unisex. On the contrary. Relativity applies here as everywhere else. What I am talking about is wholeness. Wholeness of personality; wholeness of society. The inner-space story concerns above all our exploration of gender within the personality, the operation of anima and animus, a preoccupation of folk-fairy tales all down the centuries. *Beauty and the Beast* is either a rather arbitrary story about an external reality or a very profound story about personal growth, about consummating an over-dominant and crude animus with the refining subtlety of, in this example, a nervously submissive anima so that a balanced being is born. And it has as much to do with the nature of men as of women.

The inevitable partner of that inner-space story is the outer-space story which explores the necessary social, political, moral, legal, economic, and other changes which must accompany any harmonizing of individual gender. Please do not assume that I am simply talking about women's liberation, which gets the argument right when it talks about both those realities together, and gets it wrong when it isolates only the sexual, or the anima sides of the story for attention. That is why Doris Lessing is one of our most impressive authors: the *how* of her books is in tune with the big changes we are talking about. And especially in *The Golden Notebook* she explores the inner and outer realities of dealing with discordance of genders in a story guided by a sense of an ending that envisages wholeness.

The influence of this change can already be seen in children's books, and not as a result of people demanding the propagandist benefits of apronless women and houseworking men. Let me take just one small sign. It lies in the very phrase *children's books*. In time past it was easier, indeed it was usual, to talk of books for boys and books for girls. *Treasure Island, Tom Sawyer, Coral Island* were considered books for boys. Not just in their preponderance of male characters but in the attributes of masculine gender that dominate them, we might now say they are books about maleness. *Little Women, Ballet Shoes, Anne of Green Gables* were books for girls, and feminine attributes do control them.

This is less and less the case in books written now. Into which category, for example, books for boys or books for girls, would you place the following? Betsy Byars's *The Midnight Fox*, which has a boy protagonist, and her story *The Pinballs*, which is mainly about the girl Carlie, who some might think is a masculinely domineering person. Where would you put Gene Kemp's *The Turbulent Term of Tyke Tiler*, in which the reader is allowed for almost all the book to think that the girl protagonist is a boy; or that brilliant little masterpiece by Reiner Zimnik, *The Crane*, in which a young man with a feather in his blue cap remains like Simon Stylites at the top of his crane while ages of time pass beneath him, until finally he leaves the story an old man?

As always, of course, a transcendent work from the old tradition helps enlighten the new. The example that comes to mind here, surprising us again with its modernity, is Lewis Carroll's *Alice's Adventures in Wonderland*, which might accurately be described as 'variations on the theme of gender'.

Quite simply, it would be critical folly to call any of this writing 'books for boys' or 'books for girls'. Calling them children's books, is, at present, fairly safe. But already some of us are uneasy about that, for reasons I will return to in a moment. For now, let me hope that the point is made. From our attitudes to the old fairy tales we tell to infants right through to recent work for adolescents of the order of

Alan Garner's *The Owl Service*, literature for the young is changing in its newly found self-consciousness about gender. The subject of gender becomes ever more pressing as the exit into space becomes more enticing, more obviously an historic imperative. For our life out there will depend utterly on the strength and potency of our balance of gender, and this must be achieved in our inner-space and here on Earth.

IV

We come to the fourth word on my list. Nuclear fission. Another of the results of Einstein's General Theory. Presently we are fearful of it, preoccupied by its potential evil. What is certain, for good or evil, is that nuclear fission has irrevocably changed human life. To begin with, along with Relativity and the exit into space, it has revised our sense of an ending, constraining us to face the fact that we—all of us together—are the agents of our own survival. No longer is it possible to leave everything to some God, or to ignore what goes on in other places far removed from our own homes, or to dismiss small groups of violent people, whatever their authority, as tinpot weirdos who can only do local damage. This, no author for children or anyone else can forget in his storytelling. And it is a knowledge all the more potent for being a moral knowledge, which therefore dictates a sense of direction in whatever theme he chooses to explore. The only escape is into withdrawal, into writing nostalgic fantasies about a world in which we pretend that the all-too-real potential ending does not exist.

Nuclear fission as an image also influences our ideas about Form as well as about Content. For example, nuclear fission is not linear in its pattern of action but orbicular. That is, it goes off in all directions at once, convoluting in complexity as it goes. Also, the energy is released by what we have come to think of as 'splitting the atom'. A small, apparently complete particle is, shall we say, broken open, with the result—given suitably fissionable material—that great energy is produced. And this is maintained in an expanding (as we think of it) 'chain reaction'.

To extend this image to the story form: small particulars of character and action that seem in themselves finished, complete, are, against expectation, split, and, if they are fissionable, cause a chain reaction in our imaginations, our thoughts. Thus they become nuclear reactors, breeding high-energy forms of fuel that power our interior beings. The great modern example of a nuclear novel is of course Marcel Proust's *Remembrance of Things Past* ... The transcendent example from the old tradition, which in fact exemplifies everything I have been saying here, is the work of William Shakespeare. I feel about him rather as Peter Brook does. 'Shakespeare', Brook said some years ago, 'is a model of a theatre which contains Brecht and Beckett, but goes beyond both. Our need in the post-Brecht theatre is to find a way forwards, back to Shakespeare.' We might well substitute Brook's use of the word theatre with the word literature.

All of which may seem excessively complicated: too much for children's books. But as I tried to show last year in my Woodfield Lecture, *Axes for Frozen Seas*, the great glory of Story, its magical property, is that even in the very simplest story there can be unbelievable power and nuclear energy. Some of the books I have already mentioned are like this: Zimnik's *The Crane*, Browne's *A Walk in the Park*, Sendak's work, and I expect we can all think of many more. Let's examine one example in more detail.

In *The Stone Book* Alan Garner takes one specific child belonging to one specific family on one specific day in one specific year and in one specific place. In the course of about 7500 words and in a highly polished, very 'finished' story, the child, Mary, climbs a specific church steeple (it is still there in Alderley Edge), taking a meal up to her stonemason father who is fixing a golden weathercock to the top of the spire. Later her father takes Mary into an ancient underground passage and she squeezes alone into a cavernous room where she finds marks in the stone that convey a secret message. After that, her father prepares for Mary a gift of a little book made of stone, a present she had asked for at the beginning of the story.

This is not a narrative controlled by the action of the plot, nor by the characters, but, like a poem, by the images: up the steeple; in the cavernous room; the stone book itself. And though it seems a finished object *The Stone Book* belongs to three more books, all similar in length and manner of construction. All are independently themselves, yet all are interdependent. Each one looks forward to the others and back to the ones that come before, and outward to stories that break into the quartet and pass out again, like those about the Allman family, and Uncle Charlie, and old William.

Even to begin talking about these four utterly modern books is to set off in all directions at once: family, craft, social and economic history, language, construction in stone and metal and wood, and out of words and pictures and events. On and on. Orbicular, expanding, convoluting. Yet simple, small, compact, completed.

Quite obviously the relativities of time and space, of differing points of view, and of multiple narrators are all at work. Not by accident but by design. They are not peripheral to the quartet, but integral to both its content and its form.

And what of the quartet's sense of an ending? Consider the final moment of the fourth book, *Tom Fobble's Day*. Here young William, last in the line of his family, slides on a sledge down the bankside of the very hill under which his great-grandmother, Mary of the first book, once burrowed into the cavernous room and found its secret. Tucked about him, William carries the genetic structure of all that is best in his family's history: its language, its skills, its relationship to others and the land where they live. He is wrapped against the winter snow and against the barren cold of the war going on around him, for this is 1941 and as William sledges in the night bomber planes growl above him. He is like a chrysalis enclosed in an armoured husk preparing its transformation while all about the world lies in winter's death or is busy killing itself in the cold.

Beneath the snow is the land where in the earlier books golden crops were grown, and stone was cut by careful craftsmen, where metal was wrought into intricate shapes used in the delicate balance of a clock by which to tell the time, and in the swelling belly of a weathercock by which to tell the direction of the wind. William is first met sliding on a sledge made out of the remnants of an old baby carriage once used to carry his great-grandmother Mary's babies. And it was Mary in the first book who climbed the church spire and sat on the weathercock and was spun round and round in space and was not afraid. At the other end of the story, her great-grandson hugs the earth on his sledge, waiting. The end of the *Stone Book* quartet is in its beginning, and its beginning is already pointing up and out, signalling what the clockkeeper in *The Aimer Gate* calls 'an escapement to the sun'.

The Stone Book creates a world of its own yet at the same time acknowledges that its own world is bigger than the parts of it we are shown and, just as important, that its world is not concerned with itself, but with our world—the reader's world—which we try to grasp through language. Language: when all is said and done, the subject of this quartet, at its heart, is language.

What have we so far? First, the great twentieth-century changes create three grand themes that inevitably inform any literature belonging to our time:

One: Story about the 'out there': about the struggle we are undergoing, individually and corporately, to free ourselves from our earthbound, parochial, and usually self-imposed oppressions, in preparation for our exit into space. The struggle, if you like, to absorb and transform the constraints and bedevilments of our histories.

Two: Story about 'in here': the exploration of our inner universe as we gain more and more knowledge of it. That psychic struggle itself forms and shapes our outer lives.

Three: Story about the inner- and outer-space exploration of Gender.

V

But, some people will say, these themes are common in our literature all down the ages. What is so new about them? The newness has to do with two things. First, changes in form, in the *how* of Story. Which brings me to my fifth and last word. I have written down the word Television. But what I really mean ought to be called something like 'the microelectronic book'.

Can anyone doubt that television has not already changed Story? Let me mention a few of the techniques it has made commonplace. Stop frame; replay; edit out; overlay; split screen; voice-over-picture; rapid intercutting in montage; slow motion; fast motion; rewind; separation of voice and picture so that each can deal simultaneously with content different from the other; an almost tedious dependence on dialogue.

These techniques are some of the most obvious. And now, with the arrival of videotape recorders, any child can intervene in the making of a story, can actually reconstruct it, using passages from other stories or from any recordable material he cares to choose. The viewer can become co-creator. This has extreme implications we must leave for another time to discuss; but let me draw your attention to a new Puffin book. Titled *The Warlock of Firetop Mountain* its blurb

73

announces that it is, 'Part story, part game—one in which YOU become the hero!' This is a simple form of the story-games published in such magazines as *White Dwarf*.

The significance of these publications is that they are part of a rapidly expanding and popular movement in which a writer provides the elements of a story for one or more people to construct but omits a vital chromosome from the narrative genes. He leaves out the *why*: the motivation. You, the storymaking player of the game, must not only make choices about character and action, but are responsible for the moral structure of the tale. The print forms for this activity are crude and clumsy. Within years, if not months—probably, in fact, we already have it—all this will be put on to some form of microelectronic equipment so that the players can call up both visually and verbally whatever the story-game offers and play with the results of their mutual invention in extraordinarily sophisticated and complicated ways. This does not mean that the literary book we know is at an end; it is simply an extension in our outer-space lives of what reading theorists and researchers tell us already goes on in our heads as we read. What it will do is alter the relationship of author and reader, and thus change the nature of storytelling even more.

But this development is still to come. Let's go a little deeper into what is already with us. In television, fact and fiction (to use those words in a conventionally understood sense) are shown in an unending stream that lacks any overall and coherent artistic responsibility. That is, no one decides for moral-artistic reasons that one image-programme shall follow another. And as we all know juxtaposition of images willy-nilly creates meaning.

Television says things no one intended to say. Fact adjoins fiction. Sometimes fact and fiction are intermingled within one image-programme, for the TV makers use each other's techniques indiscriminately. A play, for instance, about a runaway boy will deliberately use sequences produced to look exactly like a news broadcast in which a reporter interviews the boy's parents, and a supposed studio discussion (or a real one) about the causes of child abuse; and still photographs of children who have in actuality been battered and are not actors made up to look like them, and so on.

To some extent there is nothing new in this. Storytellers have always tried to make their tales resemble the most popular form of communication of their day. Think of Richardson's *Pamela*, which aped the letters newly literate servants were then sending each other, and of Defoe, whose *Robinson Crusoe* exploited the then popularity of travel books about distant places.

The difference with television and story is that the machine that delivers TV programmes to us is itself an entity. It is like a single book. And the flow of its narrative, comprising a mix of anything and everything available in fact and fiction and in an a-responsible stream of images, seems to become itself a single entity. So we can say that television presents us with a multi-narrated story in which there is a constantly shifting style of presentation, using an ever increasing number of techniques like those I have listed in order to bring us a multi-thematic content that flows endlessly on and is therefore ever present in our lives, both at our most private and our most public moments.

I am not suggesting that authors should copy television just because it is there. On the contrary, it is my view that authors must look for those things television cannot speak about or which it speaks about badly (like our inner-space lives, for instance, where TV is very weak indeed). What I am saying is that TV, as presently the most influentially popular means of communication, very strongly forms people's way of thinking, not simply in content but in form. Authors must make judicious use of TV techniques in their storytelling, because its techniques are a reflection of the way people now think and imagine and see the world.

TV has brought another considerable change important to us today. It is breaking down the division between child and adult. In the vast majority of British homes there is no division at all so far as TV viewing is concerned. The whole family watches everything. For authors, not to mention publishers, librarians and teachers, the implications of this state of affairs have to be attended to, for they affect both form and content, and the potentials for children's literature and its audience.

We can see some of the results of all this in children's books. Raymond Briggs's *Fungus the Bogeyman* has been much discussed in its relation to comic-strip. In fact, the influence of TV is much greater. Look at the way Briggs combines supposedly fact or informational writing and pictures with his fictional story. See how he expresses time and space relationships, how he manipulates words to pictures—sometimes like commentary, sometimes like dialogue, sometimes like authorial intrusions, sometimes like separated voice-over-picture, each dealing with different topics; and so on.

Robert Cormier's *I Am the Cheese* and *After the First Death* make skilled use of TV techniques. Indeed, *After the First Death* would easily adapt into a TV drama-documentary. Philippa Pearce's vivid little novel, *The Battle of Bubble and Squeak*, is controlled by techniques made familiar by TV handling of drama, as becomes very clear if you compare it with her earlier book *A Dog So Small*, which is much more attuned to nineteenth-century narrative modes. And Florence Parry Heide's *The Shrinking of Treehorn* is almost a TV drama in a book, with even Edward Gorey's pictures being framed and, if I may use the word, 'shot' like TV images.

Some people, I'm sure, will be thinking that I am saying that the literature of our past is dead. Not at all. What I do say is that writing now as if we were still living in the past is a dead act. Rembrandt is still wonderful, astonishing, we still learn from him, but to paint as he painted would be simply to copy. The same is true about writing like Shakespeare and Dickens and D. H. Lawrence. The old tradition is something I treasure and love; like many of you, I have spent part of my life trying to hand it on to the young. But the old tradition only remains vital, only remains alive at all, if we enlarge it, and bring into it what seems to us to be new in our world.

We are all trapped within the images of the society to which we belong. We are all members of what Stanley Fish has called 'an interpretive community' that binds us into corporately understood ways of thinking. Part of an author's responsibility is to keep on testing those images, helping us change them as our knowledge and experience grow. Thus authors help us to survive. And not just to survive into the new, but to survive with dignity, discrimination, self-awareness.

For the problem of our human world, so it seems to me, is not too much danger from individuality, but danger from too little of it; not too much danger from individual freedom, but danger from too little of it; not too much danger from people thinking for themselves and freshly, but too much danger from the interpretive community which organizes and controls every individual's potential for thought. Story is subject to those dangers, authors often seek to challenge and confront them. Children's authors are—or ought to be—in the van of those who help children, the new community, to reach beyond the tired limits of the community into which they happen to be born.

Letter
from England

From 1972 until 1984 I wrote a regular column in the American *Horn Book Magazine*. My brief was to deal with British children's books in a personal way. The Horn Book Inc. were also distributors in the U.S.A. of *Introducing Books to Children*. When a second revised edition was proposed, they took on its publication, bringing it out in 1983, and reversing the process, with Heinemann Educational Books, the original publisher, now distributing the Horn Book edition in Britain. Wanting to mark this U.S. connection here, I have chosen this piece to represent the more than fifty written during the column's twelve-year run.

*

AMERICAN WRITING AND
BRITISH READERS

There's a quality in American writing which makes it possible for some English readers to feel more at home with your literature than with their own. I'd like to try and sort out what that quality is, not only because it interests me but because it might throw some light on why American books are, on the whole, more widely read among English children than English books are read among American children.

Consider, to begin with, the following passage:

Mrs Jackson came out of the staff entrance and caught up with Donald in the drive. They walked down it in the quiet throng of exodus. The wind, lessening now, was the noisiest thing, coming up behind people and giving them sudden pushes and dodging aside when it was leaned on. Mr Braxham sailed by with his arms wide under his cloak.

'It's a great help,' he said, smiling at the ease with which he was moving along. Mrs Jackson smiled back, but only politely: the smile did not last beyond his passing or reach further than the outside of her lips.

'It'll be against him when he goes towards the vicarage,' said Donald.

'It'll be against Daddy's car,' said Mrs Jackson. Donald let the wind tune itself equally in either ear. He wanted to say something about the word 'Daddy', which he was no longer able to say easily because lately it had seemed so childish. But neither of them at home seemed to think anything was amiss with it, and all the embarrassment was his own. He wanted a quiet moment to mention it in, and this one, in the drive, was too noisy and too public. [p. 19]

And compare it with this:

If you knew I was a seventeen-year-old handsome guy hacking out this verbose volume of literary ecstasy, you'd probably think I was one of those academic genii who run home after a titillating day at school, panting to commence cello lessons. I regret to inform you, however, that I do not suffer from scholasticism of the brain. In fact, I suffer from it so little I dropped out of my puerile, jerky high school exactly eleven months ago.

About the only thing I do remember from that academic abyss is my English teacher, Mrs. Konlan, saying, when she was sober, that if you're going to write anything you can't say nasty things all the time. You're supposed to say nice things too so the story will be richer—*more balanced*, she'd say. Well, I don't totally agree with that. I think it might make this book crap. [p. 5]

You could hardly mistake the cultural origins of these two passages. The first is strictly regulated by what Richard Hoggart has accurately described as 'a confident coolness of tone, a thoroughly assured sense of the way syntax shall be made to denote just this kind of quality, this sort of attitude; there is a sense of closely prescribed and regulated communion between the author and his readers in their approach to the emotions and the way they will express them.' [p. 96] It is a tone which speaks to the reader from an assumed sharing of heritage and social background; it is very nearly haughty (or seems so to anyone outside the author's community), knows its place exactly, works through 'restraint and understatement, obliquity used as an emotional check'.

All kinds of touches give away its unconsciously held attitudes. Mr Braxham, sailing by in his priest's cloak, to whom Mrs Jackson, a teaching colleague who dislikes the man, reacts with required courtesy. But at the same time she conveys her reservations by smiling 'only politely', and the smile doesn't reach further 'than the outside of her lips'! Everything is happening, note, as a school lets out in a 'quiet . . . exodus'. Where but in a certain kind of English school do the kids leave quietly?

Then there's Donald, the protagonist, and so typical of the society about which the book is written and by whom it is intended to be read that only now in mid adolescence (he's fifteen) is he beginning to be embarrassed by the use of the word 'Daddy' but yet requires 'a quiet moment to mention it in' and not somewhere public and noisy.

What we have here is the writing of the English middle class. The signals are all hints and the style proclaims its natural home. The extract comes from *A Game of Dark* by William Mayne, and I'd wager that few American youngsters, however good they might be as readers, find themselves able to read the book with any ease or even ready understanding.

By contrast, the second passage is much more direct. To some English readers—those who feel comfortable with Mayne—it will seem strident, even cacophonous. It mixes crude rhetorical irony ('I regret to inform you, however, that I do not suffer from scholasticism of the brain') with a looseness of language that verges on the unruly and certainly the ill-disciplined ('I dropped out of my puerile, jerky high school' or 'might make this book crap'). But the quality these readers would feel most uneasy about, would shy away from, is its openness. This is writing that wears its emotions on its lapel, and among the English middle class, to do that verges on the sinful. Men have been ostracized for less. While pretending to take nothing seriously, the second passage actually takes everything far more seriously than does Mayne's. For this seventeen-year-old narrator there'd be no waiting for a quiet moment in a private place; he proclaims himself to anyone who will listen. The Mayne-English would say that the passage lacks a proper restraint, that it is cocky, overconfident. Arrogant is the word that would be used.

The passage comes, of course, from *I Never Loved Your Mind* by Paul Zindel, and among a great many English teenagers it is extremely popular and is read, along with Zindel's other books, without difficulty and with a sense of relief. So are Robert Cormier's *The Chocolate War*, S. E. Hinton's novels, Beverly Cleary's *Fifteen*, *Go Ask Alice*, Patricia Windsor's *The Summer Before*, and a surprising number of others. (I've just been looking at some American lists of 'most read' teenage books. There are very few English books included. On a similar British list a third of the titles were from the U.S.A.)

And this appeal is not restricted to teenagers. From Dr Seuss's Beginner Books, the Frog and Toad stories, and Sendak through *The Shrinking of Treehorn* and *Ramona the Pest* to *The Eighteenth Emergency* and *Little House in the Big Woods*, the number of American books that find a fairly large, and sometimes very large, British readership is considerable.

What the passage from William Mayne shows, I hope, is just how tied to the confines of its social and literary heritage the best English writing still is. And this is the very quality which makes it difficult not just for American children, but for the majority of English children too. Everything depends on the question of whom you are speaking to—and therefore of how you speak to them—rather than, as some Americans have supposed, on details like pounds and pence rather than cents and dollars, afternoon tea, and playing cricket—a point I'll return to later.

I speak from experience. I was born into the unliterary working class but given a high school education in a traditional, and therefore middle-class, grammar school. When I read English literature I feel entirely at home with Shakespeare and Donne and most work written before the mid-eighteenth century. But with work written after that, and especially with the English novel, I know I do not belong to it nor it to me. I admire it, yes; I'm proud of it, inordinately; I've learned, latish in life, how to enjoy it. But I do not feel at home with it. During my adolescence I felt comfortable with a lot of H. G. Wells. But I found myself only in D. H. Lawrence's *Sons and Lovers*, some of his short stories, and his poetry. The reason is suggested by Richard Hoggart when he remarks, in the article already quoted, that *Sons and Lovers* was, and may still be, 'the only considerable working-class novel we possess—one that is organic, unpolemical and unpatronizing'.

Throughout my teens I much preferred to read American writers. Tom Sawyer was me; Tom Brown was not me but was what I sometimes wished I could be. I adored Huck Finn and regarded *Alice in Wonderland* as a book about the people up the valley who lived in the big house, had servants and a large car, and spoke with a quite different accent from mine—an accent that seemed calculated, and was certainly used, to put me in my place.

Later, when I came across Aldous Huxley and Virginia Woolf and even dear, glorious, Irish Bernard Shaw, though I enjoyed them, I still felt like the raggy-tailed, back-street boy spying across the hedge and watching 'them' at play. And the sensation was again generated by the tone of voice; they were speaking to each other, not to me. But American writers like Hemingway in the Nick stories and some of Steinbeck brought me up against myself. For a time I thought Arthur Miller's *Death of a Salesman* the greatest play of the twentieth century, I guess because of what it said (and the way it was said) about fathers and sons and the texture of ordinary life now. And I had no doubt, and still haven't, that Eliot's *The Waste Land*—*the* poem of my youth—was so *right* not because of the influence of the late-nineteenth-century French poets, as so many of the critics seemed to say, nor of the old English poets either, but because of Eliot's American origins.

So only in D. H. Lawrence did I find a literature written by someone from my social circumstances. The discovery of him was made with a sense of astonishment, an almost overpowering excitement. At the age of fifteen and after five years' immersion in Eng. Lit., literature ceased to be a school subject and became a way of life: I actually began to desire it as one desires food and drink. When we talk about children becoming literary readers we all too often forget that this discovery is an essential part of the experience, all the more important for those not born into a literary society.

For many years, then, the roughly contemporary literature that provided my nourishment was American, not English. I believe many English children and teenagers still find this at least partly true for them. Because America is so much more a polyglot society than England and so much less specific in social class, an American writer approaches his craft differently from the way his English fellow does. The American has to establish his relationship with his audience with each book. He makes fewer, if any, class-based assumptions; there are fewer culturally narrow references, there is no confident literary élite. In any case, his literary roots, not to mention his national roots, are far less firmly entrenched. Any English writer knows his roots, and feels their grip, which is why writers who come out of the unliterary working class and pass through our education system find themselves taken over by the tone which speaks to the traditional, literate community. Lacking a closely identified audience to speak to, the American is forced (free?) to do something else. He has to establish himself, his characters, and his narrative in such a way that the reader is drawn into what he has to say.

We see this at work in the Zindel passage, the opening lines of the book. Zindel is setting up the tone and the character as quickly and as firmly as he can. We're given Dewey's age, present circumstances, and attitude to school; we understand by various signals that he is white, and we realize that he is both intelligent and articulate. Within a few pages we also know his social background. Most importantly, the style has made such an impression that we have either closed the book and left it alone or decided to accept Dewey (and Zindel) for what he is. Our own cultural position does not become an element in the story.

It is this last feature we must carefully note. English writing of the kind I have used Mayne to exemplify sets about its business by engaging the reader as an ally—social, cultural and linguistic—of the author. It assumes we know precisely what it is talking about and therefore doesn't go out of its way to explain anything. American writing, and most markedly those books which prove popular with children and teenagers here, focuses on the protagonist and the tale, both of which are offered regardless of the reader's social background. The books are much more approachable as a result, even when their specific references—to pretzels or to school grades or whatever—are unknown outside the U.S.A.

So, the reason that I and many other English readers—children and adults—find themselves at home in American literature is that it doesn't begin by alienating, but by opening itself to the reader. More than that: it is attractive because underlying its surface confidence is an insecurity which matches the English reader's own feelings in the face of his approved literary heritage. Your literature allies itself, unconsciously but nonetheless powerfully, with the newly literate Englishman's apprehension.

Given this profoundly influential quality, the breeziness of American writing, its willingness to experiment, comes as a bonus—fresh air blowing across open country. There's a sense of unrestricted energy, of fetters being broken. In American literature it is still possible to make mistakes, to be loud and crude and technically raw—just so long as behind it all there's something being said, no matter about what nor to whom. There's a take-it-or-leave-it freedom English writers are not allowed.

Nowhere is all this more clearly demonstrated than in writing for teenagers. This is something Americans do with verve and inventiveness and without embarrassment. Traditionally literate Englishmen scorn it, feel uncomfortable in the face of it. So far, we have produced either much-read but not usually very complex books which the critics regard with suspicion and distaste, or very uptight, rather tortured work like *A Game of Dark*. Interestingly, Alan Garner's *The Owl Service* is all about the very things I've been discussing. And I have always been amused to observe how difficult middle-class readers find the ending of that book. They say it mars the story and is a weakness when, in fact, it is the book's great strength. Given the social background and attitudes of Alison and Gwyn, only Roger, no matter how unattractive he is to the reader, could possibly lay the poltergeist which disturbs them all and which has been raised to haunt them by the class-based tensions that dramatize the characters' lives. Therein is the symbol of all I've been struggling to get at.

Alive
and Flourishing

A PERSONAL VIEW OF TEENAGE

LITERATURE

In 1978 Peter Kennerley asked me to contribute a chapter to his book *Teenage Reading*, giving the arguments as I saw them for books for teenagers. This was something I had been asked to do in talks many times during the previous ten years, and I hoped that writing down what I had to say might relieve me of having to say it again in public. And so it proved. I was active as a free-lance editor in publishing for secondary-school-aged readers for nearly fifteen years. 'Alive and Flourishing' is a kind of endpiece to that work.

*

I have never experienced any difficulty with the idea of literature for adolescents. On the contrary, all my working life, first as a teacher, then as an editor and author, such a literature has not only seemed necessary but possible, not only possible but *there*. It already exists: is written, published, read, and has been for a great many years. The rather curious, not to say eccentric, opposition to 'teenage books' has always, it seems to me, ducked this fact that the literature has a history. Indeed, the argument against teenage books is really only intelligent as an argument against children's and young people's books as a whole.

Let's settle the historical point first. As long ago as 1802 Sarah Trimmer, that vigorous educationalist whose *Guardian of Education* was the first journal seriously to review children's books in any systematic fashion, wrote in an article entitled 'Observations on the Changes Which Have Taken Place in Books for Children and Young

Persons' that, when discussing books published for the young, she would

> endeavour to separate them into two distinct classes, viz. Books *for Children*, and Books *for Young Persons*; but where to draw the line may be the Question: formerly, all were reckoned *Children*, till they had at least attained their *fourteenth year*. Now, if we may judge from the titles of many little volumes, compared with their contents, we have *Young Persons* of *five*, or *six years old*. However, in our arrangement (assuming the privilege of authorship) we shall, without regard to *title pages*, take the liberty of adopting the idea of our forefathers, by supposing all young gentlemen and ladies to be *Children*, till they are *fourteen*, and *young persons* till they are at least *twenty-one*; and shall class the books we examine as they shall appear to us to be suitable to these different stages of human life.
> [p. 22]

Nothing much changes: Sarah's forefathers well understood about adolescence; Sarah saw the need to separate the books into those for children and those for teenagers; and yet still we ring the changes on the argument about whether there can be or is a literature for young people! The truth is that by the time Jane Austen was composing *Northanger Abbey* (her own make-use of her adolescent pop reading) teenage books were well under way. Soon some still-remembered names and still-read examples of the form were coming out: Marryat's *Masterman Ready* in 1841; Charlotte Yonge's *The Heir of Redclyffe* in 1853; Hughes's influential *Tom Brown's Schooldays* in 1857; Kingsley's *Hereward the Wake* in 1866; Ballantyne's sequence of youthful adventures—a high point in the Victorian version of teenage travails—then Henty, of course, and on to the first of the early moderns: Talbot Baines Reed, with Henry Rider Haggard only a step behind, and Stevenson, the master, the peak of achievement, after which you either follow in the master's footsteps, as some still do, or look for refreshment, new avenues, different approaches.

In only a hundred years an honourable enough tradition was established for a literature which all through that time was only uneasily accepted, despite the amount of it written and read, of which the names I've mentioned are but a reminder. As always in every art, most of the work produced has sunk without trace, leaving the peaks to be admired.

I had not heard of Mrs Trimmer or that long historical pedigree when I attained Young Personhood. But I loved Reed, enjoyed Ballantyne, admired especially Twain's *Huckleberry Finn* and read great quantities of stuff I cannot now recall as individual books but only as a kind of emotional sludge: stories about life at sea (I had a patch of wanting to follow in my great-grandfather's mercantile footsteps), life in Africa (*Prester John* and *King Solomon's Mines* started that) and then found the greatest teenage book of them all, *Sons and Lovers*, when life changed a bit, and my reading with it. Colette with her older women making men of boys was unaccountably attractive for a while. I did not think of any of these as teenage books, of course. But I liked them because they talked about me, or so I thought. And I took note of the extra pleasure I got from the deeper attention I gave to books which connected directly with my current state of being.

Before we get too scornful of that, let's just examine our own latter-day reading. *Daniel Martin*, I have to confess, completely absorbed me for a whole week recently. By some critical standards it might be thought too long, a little self-indulgently rangey. I'll bet its editor wanted it cut. But, frankly, I couldn't care less; it could have gone on for another two hundred pages as far as I'm concerned. For why? Because it is about being middle-aged and working in the arts in England in the present time. There is a great deal, too, about the differences between England and America, about young people now, and that whole fascinating business of being born into the rural working class and educated into the declassed professional urban ways. This year I'm forty-four, am married to an American and have a fair bit to do with the U.S.A.; I was born into the semi-rural working class and was educated into the professions; I'm surrounded in everything I do by young people just into their twenties who exercise a large measure of say in what happens to my work. Is there any wonder that Daniel Martin seemed like a pal? If that's all right for me-and-literature, then it is all right for teenagers and what they want to read too.

Let me pause to clarify one point which always bedevils discussion of children's and teenage books. I do *not* believe teenage literature is *only* for children or teenagers; I do *not* believe that young people should *only* read what is published for them, and nothing else. Far from it. The sooner children and teenagers reach into the mainstream of our literature the better. But I do believe that most people will reach into it more vigorously, more willingly, and with deeper understanding of the pleasures it offers if they have encountered on the way a literature which is for them, in at least the way I've just described, and which is written and published with as much dedication and skill as is the best of the mainstream work.

I do not believe either, incidentally, that children and teenagers are different kinds of beings from adults. They are all people. The difference lies in the fact that children live at least part of their lives seeing things from a different point of view from teenagers and adults; they place the emphasis of concern and interest on different aspects of life, and so too do teenagers from children and adults. For that reason, *Catcher in the Rye*, although first published for adults, has become a standard work of teenage literature. And quite rightly; it is in teenage that the book carries most impact. Similarly, *The Mouse and His Child*, though published for children, is gradually settling down as a book most favoured in the teen years. It all has to do with an alchemy based on the elements of tone, content, point of view, thematic concerns, language and textual reference points.

Typically, the argument jams up at this point for lack of a critical apparatus commonly known to all of us interested in the subject. And we lack it because endless disparagement of the form by people who, for whatever reasons, dismiss teenage books as beyond serious interest—a bastard and unwanted hybrid—has frightened off those who are equipped with the training, skills and knowledge to build the critical approaches that might help. They wouldn't want to be thought academically retarded for handling such apparently unrespectable material. Thus work as diverse and honourable as Alan Garner's *The Owl Service*, William Corlett's trilogy beginning with *The Gate of Eden*, and Virginia Hamilton's novels (to name no more) are sometimes airily and ignorantly dismissed because they appear as books for young people.

I left myself a few paragraphs back at the classroom door. I'll pick myself up there again, but this time going in as a teacher. I have recorded some of the results of the first few years of my teaching career in *The Reluctant Reader* and will not bore you with them again. Teenage books as a bridge between children's and adult literature was the initial impelling idea behind Topliners and the beginning of my accidentally acquired career as an editor. As one Topliner reader wrote, explaining why he liked them, 'It is a big step up from Blyton to Doetovsky'. If you haven't made it by the time you are twelve you need help. That being so for the majority of people, I reasoned, why should the 'bridge books' be any less well written and produced than the mass of books in the general trade lists? Why should they be, if anything at all, self-consciously and apologetically 'educational' products, produced by people whose aims were pedagogic rather than literary, and by firms more expert in manufacturing textbooks to satisfy the peculiarities of a teacher in a classroom than in the making of books intended for the pleasure of a reader-at-home? For better or worse the result was Topliners.

Very quickly, however, I came to see that teenage literature was not simply about bridging, a kind of literary remedial course. It could do, and should do, what any literature that is whole does: grow to satisfy writers and readers in increasingly multifarious ways, responding to its own history, to other arts, and to the needs of its own time. Topliner readers led me to that recognition: to the possibilities for teenage literature. From the start they wrote letters about the books; they still arrive at the rate of a couple of dozen a week—with the occasional daunting class-load. 'Dear Editor, our teacher said we had to write and tell you what we thought of . . .' Spontaneity of response is one thing, forced marches to the post box are another.

Certain features are common to most of the willingly written letters. Let me list them. The majority like best stories which are about: people roughly their own age; contemporary times; the obvious, but none the less potent, themes: parental relationships, challenging authority, establishing one's own personality and future, relationships with peers and (when allowed in a literature still puritanically controlled by the intermediary adults) sex.

So far, so predictable; but there is a pressure point less explicitly articulated and which, writing replies to the weekly mail, one begins to feel with increasing seriousness. There is a between-the-lines statement: 'I know what I like but want to be taken further'. As a question, it is often put this way: 'Could you tell me what other books of this kind I would enjoy?' The idea that people want more of the same all the time is not actually true, I think. Not in this context at least. What they are asking for, I've learned, is not just a repetition of the pleasure but *a deepening and an expansion of it*.

A personal parallel to help make the point: I mentioned earlier my reading of *Daniel Martin*. Shortly after reading that novel I enjoyed also John Wain's *The Pardoner's Tale*, most of Iris Murdoch's *The Sea, the Sea*, and found myself then unexpectedly wanting to reread

Graham Greene's *The End of the Affair*. The overlapping connections between those books are pretty plain and—my point—I know I enjoyed each of them all the more because of the contrasting presence of the others. I would have got less from each if I had not read the others. That is a commonplace phenomenon and in my view it is an essential event in truly literary reading. All the more important, then, that young people experience it and grow literarily thereby. But to make possible an enhancing multiplicity of narratives, the books must be written, published, and be widely available: there must be a teenage literature, not just a few books that happen by chance to be especially liked by teenagers.

The need for such books I knew from my own teenage years and from my time as a teacher. The publishing possibility I learned from my work as an editor. But in the end everything depends on writers who want to write such books.

At the time of touting the idea of Topliners in the mid 1960s, I was told by all sorts of people—publishers, librarians, booksellers—that there was not only no market for teenage books but that no writers worth their muse would want to write them. It is still said. Patent nonsense, of course. The history of the form tells us otherwise. And writers working now explain why. In a letter to me later published in *The Reluctant Reader* Alan Garner, having first said he was not a children's writer, not a 'fantasy writer', not anything else but simply a writer, put his reasons like this:

> Yet I do want children to read the books, and especially do I want adolescents to find them. Simply, children make the best audience. Connect with a child and you really connect. Adolescence is the same only more so. . . . It is this thesis, that adolescence may be a form of maturity from which the adult declines, that involves me and will do so for as far ahead as I can see. [p. 105]

More recently Garner has refined that notion in an interview published in *Signal* 27, September 1978. But addressing the audience which you find most receptive for what you have to say is as legitimate a reason as any for exercising an art in a particular way. Writing in order to re-create your own adolescence and thus deal with it is another drive for some. Telling stories to connect one's own youth with one's children's present youth and the times they live in is the drive behind Robert Cormier's *The Chocolate War* and Robert Westall's *The Machine-Gunners*. And I get too many unsolicited manuscripts from people who *want*, for whatever reasons, to write *for* teenagers, to suppose for one moment that this is all a strange, aberrant and minority matter.

I can speak with most authority about myself. Leaving aside my work as a teacher and an editor, I can test all this out within my own experience as an author. I write *for* teenagers (as well as for adults and for children). This is not the place to explore the neurotic or experiential roots of that impulse; I'm simply noting it as an indisputable fact. My novel, *Breaktime*, resulted not from any calculated use of programmed formula, nor from deliberate invention to satisfy the postal votes on reading preferences that come from Topliner readers. In this limited and self-conscious sense, the story was not made; it happened. And while it was happening everything else to do with teenage literature was forgotten. All I knew before, during, and after the event, was that I had to get the story down in this way, and that if anyone else was to read it, I would most prefer that anyone to be an adolescent. It was about the adolescent-still-in-me and it was for the adolescent-still-in-the-reader.

If I had wanted the book to connect with the adult-in-me, I would have done it differently. There would have been a shift in the point of view, changes in the assumed and explicit references. In short, the tone and the rhetoric of the book would have been handled another way. What those differences consist in—what makes a book *for* teenage or not—is a fascinating topic, the one we really ought to be discussing, rather than continuing the wearying argument about whether teenage books can or ought to exist. But, as I said before, we cannot explore such topics without a critical apparatus that helps us do so. The raw material for that critique is already available in great quantity. Forging it into a coherent body of work is but an academic's sinecure away. And if anything needs to be done to better the status and innovatory progress of teenage literature, that's it. For a healthy critical atmosphere stimulates writers and publishers, opens up their work to associated professionals (librarians and teachers) and thus clarifies the form and its reception.

Apart from this, the real problem about teenage literature is not whether it ought or ought not to exist—as I've said, it does and isn't about to go away—but is a question of availability to the readers. The problem is not, therefore, literary but commercial. Librarians still haver anxiously about what to do with the books and where to put them; teachers in secondary schools and colleges are still often lamentably ignorant of what has been produced, and in their ignorance adopt censorial prejudices against the very idea of the books. And while those powerful bodies of buyers-on-behalf-of-teenage-readers remain so confused, publishers hesitate in identifying clearly which of their books belong to the category. So far, in contrast to the state of things in a number of other countries, only The Bodley Head has had the courage to nail their colours to the mast and declare what is what on their list. That is something for which writers like myself feel grateful—I would not have wanted *Breaktime* to appear unmarked on a children's list. Of the paperbackers, only Penguin, aside from the Topliner list, have tried, somewhat nervously to judge from their choice, to gather their teenage forces in the erratic Peacock list. [Since 1978, Penguin have initiated their Puffin Plus list and other, originating publishers have added teenage lists to their range.]

The aim for the future then must be, in my view, to clarify the form critically, and to tidy up and invigorate the distributive channels. The books themselves, against those presently undermining odds, continue to grow rapidly in number and to develop in nature.

Ways of Telling

FROM WRITER TO READER: AN

AUTHOR READS HIMSELF

A lecture given at the University of Stockholm in May 1984 is the basis of the following conflation of other talks and lectures given over recent years in various places: the U.S.A., Canada, Australia and Israel.

*

You have been kind enough to ask me to speak about the ways of telling, and specifically the narrative structures, of my novels. Before doing so, I'd like to distinguish between the three-persons-in-one who stands before you. (If this sounds dangerously like a claim to triune godhead, you will, I'm sure, be very soon relieved of any anxiety on that score.)

Here stands, most obviously, the person who breathes, eats, behaves, generally speaking, in a manner recognizable as biologically human, lives with a woman called Nancy and, as Wayne Booth says it in his everlastingly useful *The Rhetoric of Fiction*, 'goes about paying bills, repairing leaky faucets, and failing in generosity and wisdom'. Then, you also see before you the man who writes books and finds to his surprise and gratification that he manages to make a living from what is for him an imperative occupation. Inside these two stands another, third person, a reader who gains the greatest, though not the only, pleasure of life from reading other people's writings.

It is this third person, the reader, who must speak to you today. For the author of the books is dead, a person who belongs to the past. Roland Barthes, that elegant and pluralist critic, tells us that 'the birth of the reader is at the cost of the death of the author', and my whole experience of writing and of reading convinces me this is true. The books are finished events; the person who wrote them is no more. He has a biography, as the writing of his books has a history. But he has no extra-textual presence, and the books, as texts, stand on their own, having a life independent of their author, but dependent for their continued existence on the readers who make them their own.

When I speak to you as a reader, therefore, I speak only as one reader among many, whose reading is no more important than any other's. Let me also acknowledge that all reading is an act of translation; and that all reading is an act of interpretation. I mention this in order to reassert the unique quality of everyone's reading, but for a more mundane reason as well. I shall be referring to my reading of the English-language editions of my books. I'm quite sure that your Swedish editions, as will be true of the German, French, Dutch, and others, are different in significant ways, not only because of the language problems of translation, but because each other-language edition is to some extent a reader's interpretation of the original.

This by way of preface. Now for an introduction. You ask me to speak about the narrative structure of my books. The words *narrative structure* are much used these days, seeming to countenance a variety of assumed meanings. We therefore need grounds for agreement about what I, at least, mean. My guide is Gérard Genette's clarification in his essential book, *Narrative Discourse*, where he recognizes three meanings and boils them down thus:

> analysis of narrative discourse as I understand it constantly implies a study of relationships: on the one hand the relationship between a discourse and the events that it recounts . . ., on the other hand the relationship between the same discourse and the act that produces it, actually (Homer) or fictively (Ulysses). . . . Analysis of narrative discourse will thus be for me, essentially, a study of relationships between narrative and story, between narrative and narrating, and (to the extent that they are inscribed in the narrative discourse) between story and narrating. [pp. 26, 27 and 29]

Following Genette, I shall talk about the relationship between myself as storyteller (craftsman), my fictive protagonists (Ditto in *Breaktime*, Hal in *Dance on my Grave*), the events that compose their stories, and the ways of telling that produce the narrative.

Various critical insights inform what follows; most of us, I'm sure, own them. Allow me to recognize our sharing of them by quoting the words that, for me, provide their best expression. The first is from Hans-Georg Gadamer in *Truth and Method*, the others from Roland Barthes' essays in *Image-Music-Text*.

> Not occasionally only, but always, the meaning of a text goes beyond its author. [p. 264]

> . . . the work can be held in the hand, the text is held in language. [p. 157]

> We know now that a text is not a line of words releasing a single 'theological' meaning (the 'message' of the Author-God) but a multi-dimensional space in which a variety of writings, none of them original, blend and clash. The text is a tissue of quotations drawn from the innumerable centres of culture. [p. 146]

> To read (to listen to) a narrative is not merely to move from one word to the next, it is also to move from one level to the next. [p. 87]

A last quotation from Barthes serves as bridge from introduction to main theme:

> . . . the metaphor of the Text is that of the *network*. [p. 161]

The network that composes the structure of *Breaktime* is fairly easy to draw as a diagram which can be read either two-dimensionally, like a theme-catching fishnet, or three-dimensionally, like a geological section through a thematic landscape. (See next page.)

This perhaps makes the book look foggy, far more difficult for readers than I hope it is. A walker across the countryside should be able simply to enjoy the immediately visible sights without bothering to wonder how they got to be like that. In crafting a story an author strives to provide the surface with an entertaining landscape and a path pleasant enough to satisfy uninquisitive readers. But all paths, all landscapes, acquire their features and contours from a geology that lies hidden beneath the ground. Some walkers enjoy investigating these foundations, as do some readers in their enjoyment of novels. I must suppose you are that kind of reader or you would not be here today. Were I less confident of this I certainly would not risk drawing such a diagram or proceed to tell the story it depicts.

BREAKTIME:
The Network of the Narrative

Column headings:
- Boy on a 'rite of passage' adventure
- Cliché: the clichés of teenage fiction
- The structure of Shakespeare's comedies
- Underpinning folk tales and 'place': location
- Linguistic performance as a fictive act
- The question of the narrator
- Reshaping the author's own youth

Row headings:
- Fathers and sons: independence & freedom
- The novel as book; book as object
- Personally: how do we know who we are?
- Friendship: sons and lovers
- Boys and girls
- Boys and boys: we are what we envisage
- Reality as image: writing and reading
- Author and Reader

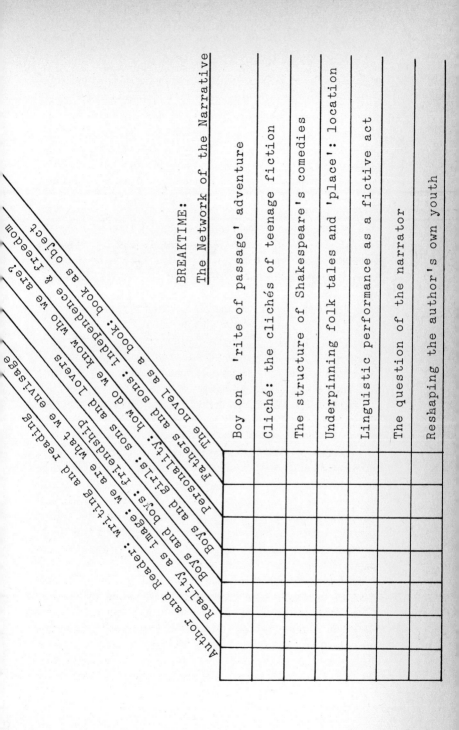

Breaktime's story turns on the axis of two intersecting 'surfaces'. The one is the plot about a boy on a journey, a rite-of-passage adventure that takes Ditto from emotional confusion to a moment of clarity and stasis, when he sits waiting, ready for the next surge in his life. The other, intersecting seam is the reader's adventure over the surface of the page, which presents the story as a graphematic, as well as a linguistic, experience—the type itself, drawings, handwriting, footnotes, 'concrete' prose, and the like—in which the novel as a book, and the book as a made object decorated with marks, becomes the focus of attention, of enjoyment I hope, and is itself one of the ways of telling the story.

These two elements—diachronic, polymodal, cruciform—set up the warp and weft of the network. They also establish the relationship between protagonist and reader, who, adventuring together, each the hero of the story, encounter one another in the printed marks on the page.

An aside. I'm aware of mixing my metaphors. I don't, however, think of them as an inappropriate soup, but as interdependent, all part of a kaleidoscope of images, no one of which is sufficiently suggestive of how a novel behaves to satisfy me on its own. Besides, as a writer and as a reader I do actually think of a novel as a pattern of three-dimensional shapes, also as music, and as a journey through space (landscape) and through multiplicities of time. And I am here giving as nearly as I can a truthful account of my reading of myself, even at risk of inelegant collisions in the kaleidoscope of metaphor.

If we now move down a level, we find a layer of soft clay: the clichés of teenage fiction. Boy meets girl; son rebels against parents; adolescents engage in rivalries and dares and the thrills of first, surreptitious sex. We find an owl hooting, cliché symbol of death; a cuckoo calls, cliché herald of a-morality; Helen, that cliché temptress, appears before Ditto dressed quite explicitly as a 'desirable cliché' when they meet for the seduction in that cliché of romantic settings, a beautiful hillside.

Cliché fascinates me. If, as is said so often it is itself a cliché, there are no new stories, then, in a crude sense, there are only clichés from which to begin. And, as with all clichés, there is some truth in this one. Barthes refines the idea by writing, 'The text is a tissue of quotations drawn from the innumerable centres of culture'. Straw and clay are clichés of earth. There are those who make of them bricks for building new places. The new is made out of the old, and the raw material is often worn out, used up as far as its original purpose goes. In cliché, the content remains true but the expressing form is exhausted. No new truths, just fresh—or refreshed—ways of expression.

Refreshment, reinvigoration, making the known new is achieved by a re-examination, a reworking, of form. So the most popular clichés are interesting because their popularity attests to their general appeal. And form preoccupies me because in form I discover energy. For me, form—the way of telling—is a composition of *voice* (the personality of language) and *craft* (the techniques by which language is given narrative expression).

All very well, however, being interested in cliché and listing off those that locate in *Breaktime*, but every story requires a plot, a framework of event that gives it shape and direction. After much fussing about at the note-making stage, when I tried to find a plot by my own unaided invention, I at last stumbled across this passage in *The 'Revels' History of Drama in English*, where Alvin Kernan writes:

> The characteristic Shakespearean comic plot extends this perpetual hesitation between dream and thought into action. As the play progresses, the characters move, in response to their own psychic urgencies and the great powers that flow through their worlds, from familiar, well-lighted places and states of mind, into strange, unfamiliar dim places and experiences, only to return after a period of confusion, surprise and revelation to their place of origin. The movement is, to use Shakespeare's most persistent symbols, from city to wood and back to city again . . . from everyday to holiday and back to everyday, from the restraints of society and order to release and freedom and then, renewed, back to work and sobriety . . . from an old society which has become repressive, tyrannous and life-destroying to a revolutionary explosion, usually undertaken by youth in the name of freedom and vitality, leading to a second period of disorder and excess. This phase gives way in turn to the formation of a new society, which, while including all within its feasts and celebrations, is centred on youth and the new generation. [p. 308]

This gave me precisely what I was looking for. Always follow the masters! I would use the standard comic plot of Shakespeare's transcendent plays, and so link *Breaktime* into the best of the English tradition, while providing myself with a blueprint for my story. Young people in rebellion against waning adult authority go off to a magic place inspiring of uninhibited, even licentious behaviour, where they discover themselves more profoundly than before, after which they return, changed and closer to achieving their personal independence, to the regulation and order of the adults from whom they will shortly take over the running of society.

Discovering this controlling design led me to ask the questions that were drillheads cutting into the next layer, a level deeper in the story's geology. Where would the story happen? Which town would be Shakespeare's 'city', which area his enchanted 'forest'?

Many years ago, an experienced writer gave me her working rule. Always write about things you know, she told me, and always write about places you know. Recalling this, I started looking at the area round my present home in Gloucestershire, but wasn't happy with it as the novel's setting. I tried other familiar locations but none was right. Finally, I thought about the part of the North East of England where I grew up, the town of Darlington, and the hills and dales round Richmond in Yorkshire.

Given the nature of *Breaktime* you might wonder why I didn't use this setting in the first place. For two reasons. The first was simply practical. I don't much like travel, Darlington is two hundred and forty miles from my home, and I didn't want the trouble of driving there every now and then to check the facts of the location. The second reason was psychological. I feared that setting the story in the places where I spent my youth might bring my own life and the fictional lives of my characters dangerously close together. I wanted to avoid the snare always waiting for novelists, the temptation to evade problems of invention by disguising autobiography as fiction. In the event, the use of my youthful stamping ground repaid the risk by giving me an unexpected and invaluable experience that has ever since been useful to me, as I'll relate in a moment.

What finally persuaded me to settle for Darlington and Richmond was the narrative potency I discovered they possessed when I imagined Ditto's story taking place there. To begin with, Darlington is flat, rather dull, architecturally undistinguished, and has a history associated with locomotives (the George Stephenson works were there) and the now dying glories, if glories they ever were, of the industrial revolution. What better correlative for the fading powers of adult authority and mores against which my young protagonist was to

98

rebel? On the other hand, the little market town of Richmond, and the Pennine valley of the river Swale at the foot of which Richmond stands guard, is scenically dramatic, outstandingly beautiful, possessively enchanted, a very type of Shakespeare's Forest of Arden. Swaledale literally sparkles with energy, for the valley is dominated by the fast-flowing, boulder-strewn, lightflecking river beside which hills stride and tumble, rise and fall again and again, like topographic athletes with big muscles. Hills and river, the male and female of geography, lying together, have conceived a landscape of vigour and beauty. What more magic place, what more likely setting to release and re-form pent-up adolescent emotions?

I knew that it would because it did that for me many years ago. The invaluable authorial experience this setting gave me, which I mentioned a moment ago, was discovering how to find in myself and in my own life reference points for truth by which to test the veracity of a character's experience during the writing of a novel. It taught me how to use autobiography in the creation of a fiction without turning the fiction into autobiography. In other words, it taught me how to use myself to write truth in fiction while also keeping my distance. I don't say I can always do it, only that taking the risk showed me what fictional truth really means.

Dig deeper, to the next level, and we find that Richmond offers not only a topography that supports the story but a typology too. Five local legends—five popular folk tales—are alive in the area. I was astonished by the closeness of match between their symbolic significance and the needs of my story. Absorbing these tales into the underground of the book gave the story a richness and a focus it till then had lacked.

These are the tales:

Robin Hood, who, as every British schoolchild knows, robbed the rich and gave to the poor, and was in fact a political dissident, was imprisoned—that is, made socially and politically impotent—in Richmond Castle for a time. The old spelling of Hood is Hode, the surname given in *Breaktime* to Robby, whose impotent rebellion against his father is expressed openly in disagreements about politics and covertly through disapproved-of sexual behaviour with his friend Jack.

In the second story, a man called Potter Thompson finds his way underneath Richmond Castle where King Arthur's knights lie asleep under a huge bell. If the bell is rung, the knights will wake and come

99

to England's aid in time of need. Potter Thompson almost rings the bell, but fails in courage. An old ballad gives his son's name as Jack. Jack Thompson is the name of Robby Hode's drop-out friend, big of body but slight of spirit, who ducks out of the brawl at the political meeting where Robby tries to rouse the members of the socialist party from their unprotesting acceptance of the sell-out of their ideals represented by their main speaker, the man we later learn is Robby's father.

A third legend tells how a little drummer boy was ordered into an ancient tunnel that was rumoured to link Richmond Castle with Easby Abbey two or three miles down river, thus connecting the now ruined political stronghold to the now ruined religious centre of the region. In order to plot the course of the tunnel the boy was told to walk through it, beating his drum loudly, while the adults listened on the ground above and followed his track. The boy did as he was told, was heard drumming for a while, but then the noise ceased and he was never heard or seen again. Ditto, you'll recall, meets Robby and Jack in Richmond Castle, attends in drunken state the political meeting in a bleak market hall—which in fact stands hard by and virtually beneath the castle—is knocked out during the brawl, and wakes, being sick into the Swale near Easby Abbey, after which he takes part in the burgling of the Hodes' house. The paralleling of the Drummer Boy's story and these incidents is all the more obvious if connections are made between, for example, the various meanings of the verb 'to drum', which include 'to sound a summoning call', 'to obtain agreement or help', 'to inform or warn off', 'to sound out or discover the truth about'.

These three tales help locate the relationships between the characters, the events, and the themes I intend.

The fourth story is given a more explicit entrance into the novel and is about the lass of Richmond hill, subject of one of the best known folk songs in English:

On Richmond hill there lives a lass
More bright than Mayday morn . . .

Here is cliché indeed, and in its most delightfully virulent form, the pop song! This lass, like so many in pop songs, is an idealization of a masculine fantasy. A variant story tells us that her real-life model was a high-class whore with rotten teeth and bad breath. But was she?

There's no indisputable evidence, and the variant story might perhaps be the work of a satirical misogynist or, for that matter, of some joyless female encratite out to score a point. At any rate, she brings with her an ironic ambiguity that pleases me and benefits Ditto's story.

How, though, to absorb it? Who, I asked, is the classic cliché of the same type? The answer was obvious: Helen of Troy, she whose face launched a thousand ships, a reputation itself the punning butt of schoolboy jokes. So Ditto's enticing lass (and possible male fantasy?), who first takes possession of him and then abandons him, became Helen, sender of snapshots and siren-song letters.

And on which hill should they sport, there being so many? This was easily decided by another local story, the fifth: well documented, more news item than legend, and openly recounted in the novel without disguise from the original sources (thus also helping create Barthes' 'multi-dimensional space in which a variety of writings, none of them original, blend and clash'). The hill is the one where Robert Willance's runaway mount, galloping recklessly through fog, plunged over a sheer scarp above the Swale, and died where she fell, leaving her rider so helpless with a broken leg that the only way he could save himself was by slitting open the horse's belly and laying his wounded leg inside to keep warm till rescue came. Afterward, he erected a monument to his horse in gratitude. No need, I think, to point out the relationship between this story and Ditto's as he and Helen ride each other beside the monument to Willance's leap on the swelling hills above the Swale, up river from Richmond.

These stories interweave, of course; they aren't separate threads. And therefore they influence and change each other as well as Ditto's narrative. To take just one example. At the political meeting where the boys sit together, drunken Ditto—having already 'drummed' Hode and Thompson—first thinks that he is in a dungeon, then that he is at a prayer meeting. When he asks, in his inebriated confusion, whether everyone is asleep, Robby tells him that they are 'wakers asleep' who are dreaming. In this brief exchange the three subventing folk tales work together, creating a subtext that draws another pattern of the book's meanings. Immediately afterwards comes Ditto's most uninhibitedly anarchic moment described in devices that also bring the graphematic features to their climax. And all this happens at the very centre of the physical book.

If the metaphor of the text is changed from a network to a wheel, this passage may be seen at the hub, with all this implies about the book's construction and the way it asks to be read. The shape is not linear, not a trajectory, like a ball being thrown from one person to another, but orbicular, like being at the centre of the wheel while it is spinning along the ground.

The last three layers take us below the structural formalities, deep into the bedrock on which the novel is constructed, where we discover the controlling themes. These extend beyond the confines of *Breaktime*, and because they are not structural but are wholly thematic in function they lie, strictly speaking, outside our discussion today. However, so important are they in my own reading of the book that for satisfaction's sake I would like to say something about them.

Quite obviously, the story plays with the relationship between so-called fiction, so-called fact, and language. Is Ditto telling 'the truth' or has he invented the story? Can Morgan or we, the readers, *know* someone else's experience except through the language in which it is communicated? What are we dealing with, what are we experiencing, when we engage in the reading of a narrative? What does fictive language *do*? Once again Roland Barthes says it best:

> The function of narrative is not to 'present', it is to constitute a spectacle still very enigmatic for us but in any case not of a mimetic order . . . Narrative does not show, does not imitate; the passion which may excite us in reading a novel is not that of a 'vision' (in actual fact, we do not 'see' anything). Rather, it is that of meaning, that of a higher order of relation which also has its emotions, its hopes, its dangers, its triumphs. 'What takes place' in a narrative is from the referential (reality) point of view literally *nothing*; 'what happens' is language alone, the adventure of language, the unceasing celebration of its coming. [*Image-Music-Text* pp. 123, 124.]

Breaktime makes no attempt to engage in discussion of these ideas; rather it makes a story out of them. And quite literally that story is only—is nothing but—language. It is a story about language and about kinds of language, and has no reality, for me, except as language.

Even Ditto's name signals that this is so. 'Ditto' means a repetition symbolized by two small marks (ʼʼ). He is, therefore, simply a drawing, marks on a page, just as his story is nothing but writing. In a literal sense, all writing is drawing, having no reality except in the marks themselves. Thus Ditto is, as a ditto sign, a tautology, a self-sustaining being who exists by indicating his own repetition. But a repetition of whom? Of no one, of course, except the being created by the language that composes his story and therefore Ditto himself. When thought of this way, a ditto mark could be said to be the most abstract of linguistic signs. It functions as a signifier to a signified that is another language, the language of Story itself. Which means that Ditto himself is a literary joke, just as his entire story is a comedy. And yet a reviewer in the London *Times* could only find in Ditto's name: 'Chambers/Ditto (get the joke?)'. The incompetence of that reading only shows once again how readers make what they like of any writing and try to crudify fiction into a poor disguise for the author's own first-person life, no matter how hard the author works to make a story's independent being clear. Nor, by the way, can the *Times* reviewer have been at all familiar with Lewis Carroll (not a sin but possibly a misfortune for anyone working on a newspaper, where familiarity with nonsense is a daily requirement), not to have remembered this scene from *Through the Looking-Glass*:

> 'I'm afraid he'll catch cold with lying on the damp grass,' said Alice, who was a very thoughtful little girl.
>
> 'He's dreaming now,' said Tweedledee: 'and what do you think he's dreaming about?'
>
> Alice said, 'Nobody can guess that.'
>
> 'Why, about *you*!' Tweedledee exclaimed, clapping his hands triumphantly. 'And if he left off dreaming about you, where do you suppose you'd be?'
>
> 'Where I am now, of course,' said Alice.
>
> 'Not you!' Tweedledee retorted contemptuously. 'You'd be nowhere. Why, you're only a sort of thing in his dream!'
>
> 'If that there King was to wake,' added Tweedledum, 'you'd go out—bang!—just like a candle!'
>
> 'I shouldn't!' Alice exclaimed indignantly. 'Besides, if *I'm* only a sort of thing in his dream, what are *you*, I should like to know?'
>
> 'Ditto,' said Tweedledum.
>
> 'Ditto, ditto!' said Tweedledee.

Language must be uttered before it can be heard. Naturally, therefore, a whole stratum of the narrative's geology, the next level down, is composed of the hard-rock questions: Who is telling this story? Whose voice do we hear? Who is the narrator?

I wish we had time to dig into these puzzles, for they are the ones that presently fascinate me about the writing of fiction. For the moment I'll only note that the use of first- and third-person voices in *Breaktime* was not arbitrary, and that the choice of voice for each passage was considered from a number of points of view, mostly to do with the problem of the narrator rather than the technical reason that the first-person creates an effect of immediacy and closeness to the protagonist while the third-person creates a sense of distance, of being an observer rather than a participant. The juxtaposing of the voices is meant to help compose a polyphony, and a duality of personality, so that the reader stands now within, now without, the story, and 'hears' the linguistic shifts more keenly than would be the case without the use of this device. (Specialist critics will know that Gérard Genette's chapter on 'Voice' in *Narrative Discourse* lays out the principal ideas that group around this element in fiction, where he searches from Proust the authorial impulse behind extradiegetic and heterodiegetic usage.)

Breaktime is sometimes criticized for being, as it is usually put, 'too self-conscious'. Agreed, there is a kind of self-consciousness that is a weakness, where the writing has not been sufficiently absorbed by the author. If this is the case with *Breaktime*, it is certainly flawed. But there are other kinds of self-consciousness. One kind has to do with the self-consciousness of teenagers like Ditto when they try to write. They imitate their favourite authors and are sometimes pompous; they over-decorate and look for unusual words and modes of expression. They also mix linguistic conventions. This kind of self-consciousness is so typical of a boy like Ditto that no writing that is supposed to be his can avoid it. Finding this style, finding *his* voice, was important to me. Another kind of self-consciousness has to do with writing that leads the reader to witness the writing itself, to be aware of it and attend to it for its own sake. Devices like mixing first- and third-person, and some of the graphematic features are designed in part to achieve this.

Move down another layer and we reach the most difficult topic of all for me to say anything about, not least because I'm still unclear about it myself. At this level is confronted the relationship that inevitably exists between the three elements: the fictive act as a linguistic performance; the person of the narrator; and the author himself in his first-person existence. Again we might pose the problem in questions: What has the author given the book? What has the book given the author? Or: Where am I in this book and what am I doing in it?

Judging from the inordinate interest there is in the biography of writers, which often exceeds interest in their books, I suspect a lot of people find this the subject that engages their curiosity most of all. But, as I say, it isn't part of our discussion today so I'll leave it alone, with this one hint. I sometimes think that what I was doing in *Breaktime* was shaping—or rather re-shaping—my own youth, re-examining it in the light of the years since then. But this is tentative and inadequate, and is offered only as a talking point for those determined to pursue biographical lines of inquiry.

Now we can shift from the vertical to the horizontal axis of my diagram. We can take that walk I mentioned earlier through the landscape of the story, following Ditto, and looking for the tributary narratives that, flowing together, make up the whole novel.

Very quickly, on the third page, we encounter the feature I've already talked about as the other main surface of the book: the graphematic elements that engage the reader's attention on the novel as a book, and on the book as a physical object covered with decorative, meaning-communicating marks. We find Morgan's type-writer-written document. Soon after we read Ditto's first interior monologue, then comes Helen's handwritten letter, the italic/roman dialogue between Ditto and his mother, and so on.

Having set out on the adventure with print, we come next to the narrative that explores the story about fathers and sons and the struggle between them caused by the natural desire of the teenage son for his independence in the face of his father's sense of parental duty and love, which Ditto now finds overbearing and restrictive.

Ditto goes to his room and the third narrative begins, the one dealing with the subject of personality. What are we? How do we know what we are? How do we make ourselves into what we wish to be? How do we perceive—how do we *know*—our lives? We look at Ditto's room, we see him as he sees himself, through the objects with which he has surrounded himself in his own territory, and which now irritate him because they reveal a person he no longer feels he is or wants to be. This narrative is about states of being. What is it like to be Ditto? What is his state of being as he experiences each event in his life?

I have elsewhere tried to explain that *Breaktime* is not so much about event or character as it is about states of being: the state of being adolescent, the state of being a son and a would-be lover, the state of being drunk and of being an amateur burglar, of being a seducer and of being seduced, and so on. Just as Shakespeare's comic plot controls the overall narrative pattern, so the examination of each episode as a state of being controls the narrator's focus of attention. This determines what he chooses to tell about, and how he tells about it.

Thus, for example, during the political meeting, the scene is produced linguistically and graphematically in such a way as to convey what it is like to be Ditto mildly drunk at such a gathering, rather than to describe to the reader what happened and why, along with some narrative comment to illuminate the meaning, which would be the more familiar (readerly) convention. In my (writerly) telling, the reader must play the game of putting the pieces together for him/herself, making the meaning that the telling signals but doesn't assert.

Later, during the seduction on the hillside, there are three narratives in one. You'll recall that the scene is printed in two columns, and that in one column the two narrative voices, the first-person and the third-person, talk simultaneously. The third-person—the voice that makes the reader stand back and think—describes the action and is set in roman type. (The German edition prints this in red, a nice touch!) The first-person, Ditto's own involving voice, is printed in italic and tells us what Ditto is thinking during the event. The facing column is entirely taken up by an extract from Dr Spock's *A Young Person's Guide to Life and Love*, in which Spock says there isn't much point in trying to describe lovemaking because it is experienced as emotion and relationship rather than as action. Having said this, he goes on to describe sexual action in considerable detail. Placed alongside Ditto's narrative the two inter-act, turning one another into comedy.

In order to understand the scene you have to read it three times. Each time—or so I hope—it gets funnier, the action less erotic, and your attention is more and more fixed on Ditto's state of being.

But these examples have taken us away from the search for the narrative's tributaries. Immediately after observing Ditto in his room and beginning the exploration of his personality, we meet Helen through the medium of her handwritten letter and Ditto's first-person monologue as he leers at her provocative photograph. Though first hinted at in Morgan's opening line, 'I tell you no lie, Maureen Pinfold is a dream,' (cf. also the reference to *Alice*, above), this is the first substantial statement of the story about boys and girls and would-be lovers that equals in importance the story about fathers and sons. Blended together they can be relabelled 'sons and lovers', a not-unconscious echo of D. H. Lawrence's novel, a formative book in my own life as in the lives of many of my generation and others since.

Having contemplated images of Helen, with disturbing results, Ditto lays alongside hers an image of Morgan—the 'Charges against literature'—and then surveys them in relation to images of himself, the objects in his room. He thus draws the main stories together, adding at the same time the one already assumed in the first page and soon to surface again the next day, when Ditto relates to Morgan the drama of his row with his father and reconsiders what Morgan, 'his friend stretched at his side', means to him. This is the story of friendship, boy with boy, which *Dance on my Grave* takes up and develops. It is of course a variation on the sons and lovers theme.

We're now taken into the story of the book as a construct of images, of fiction as metaphor. Ditto's 'Document'—his reply to Morgan's 'Charges'—sets up questions about reality as image. While above and around, extra-textually so to speak, questions are being posed between author and reader: What is fiction and what is fact? How much of what we read about Ditto is fiction (that is, lies), and how much is 'true'? How true is this 'fiction' in a sense that speaks beyond words like 'fact' and 'fiction'? Thus the vista at the end of our journey through the novel lays out for contemplation the relationship between author and reader, writing and reading. How do we view each other? What have we done with this book, and what has it done for us?

This completes the network of the text, at least when we read according to this metaphor. It makes a grid of squares, like a virgin crossword, inviting readers to play some kind of game on it. We might, for example, play a game of 'Connections'. Three along, four down: What is the connection between the boys and the underpinning folk tales, and how does this connection illuminate each? Five along and five down: What is the connection between the personality of Ditto and the linguistic performance of the book? Two along, two down: What is the connection between cliché and our image of reality?

But stop, stop! This is beginning to sound much too much like an Eng. Lit. examination paper for comfort. All the same, it is suggestive of speculation, of different ways of entering into, and considering, the book's potential meanings. Certainly, it emphasizes again that the book is not simply a linear structure. It wants to be, let's say, a hologram rather than a snapshot—a three-dimensional mobile, not a two-dimensional still.

So much for the hidden structure of the book. The visible architecture arranges the story into chronologically ordered episodes, each with its own, always signposting title. These are further grouped into four parts. I think of these as the four acts of a drama. They too are signposted by titles that suggest keynotes. The first, 'Challenge', indicates the fictional challenges issued between Ditto and Morgan, Ditto and his father, Helen and Ditto. But it also indicates the challenge issued between author and reader, and between Ditto and the reader, as an act of writing and of reading. 'Journey Out' speaks of more than Ditto's journey outwards from home, outwards from his inhibited self. It speaks also of the reader setting out on the reading journey. And so on.

This four-part pattern is further organized into eight dramatic climaxes. But the climaxes are not regularly distributed, which would have been monotonously symmetrical. The rhythm is actually: two, three, one, two. This pattern places the eventful dramatic weight in the first half of the book, and on the fourth climax. That is, on the second climax in the second part: the political brawl. This is the peak of the novel's rebellious drama and is placed right at the physical centre of the book, acting as a kind of hub.

After this, before and during the burgling of Hode's house, which doesn't carry the same action-full punch as the political brawl, Ditto 'comes to his senses'. The rest of the book is occupied with his 'happy revolution' in which he 'comes together' again, renewed, his boyness and girlness unified in the climax with Helen, his female surrogate.

You will agree, I think, that this is not the usual disposition of dramatic forces in a novel. For one thing, it places a great deal of trust on the interest readers find in the happy coming together of a character, as against their interest in confusion, disruption, and eventful action. For another, it disregards the conventional storyteller's wisdom that the dramatically strongest scene should be kept till near the end, and be followed by a rapid resolution before the reader gets bored. My arrangement was not, however, worked out as a demonstration of some theory of composition. Quite the contrary. The story dictated its own shape. My job as author, having been given the story, was to clarify the shape by removing clutter. Only after I'd completed a draft did I realize how the structure was built.

An aside. I say 'having been given the story'. This raises the distinction between authoring and writing. Being a writer is like being a furniture-maker or a cook, or any other skilled craftsperson. A furniture-maker constructs tables or chairs to a predetermined design and to satisfy a known customer. The result may be elegant or ugly, carefully done or bodged. Similarly, writers choose stories they'll write, plan them, working to known patterns, and judge their success by customer satisfaction as expressed in sales. The result may be compulsively readable or unengaging and tedious. Most books, most novels, are produced this way. It is an honourable and sometimes very lucrative trade.

But it should not be confused with authoring. Authors are like sculptors. It is an advantage if they possess, or at least know about, the craft skills of the writer, just as it is an advantage if a sculptor can employ the skills of a stonemason or a metalworker. But there are examples of revered and classic authors who clearly lacked, or didn't care about, some of the craft skills. James Joyce, it seems to me, wasn't very interested in the kind of craft skill that can make a story into a suspenseful narrative that keeps readers eager to know what will happen next. D. H. Lawrence could be, frankly, sloppy in his plotting, as well as sometimes saying far too much about a scene (an excess of Genette's paralepsis). Authors quite often seem unconcerned about passages that to a 'good' writer appear shockingly flawed. The fact is their concerns are different, their standards of judgement guided by criteria other than the ones successful writers live by.

Writers choose the stories they tell, authors are chosen by their stories. Writers look at their work from the point of view of their readers, authors look at theirs from the point of view of the story they tell. Writers seek financial reward, and regard their work as a way of making a living and perhaps of achieving social prizes like fame. Authors, though not averse to financial and social rewards, seek in literature a way of life. Writers exercise choice. Authors submit to a dedication which can also be called a neurotic obsession. Writers *may*, but authors *must* write.

Roland Barthes, in a discussion of authors and writers on differrent lines from mine, says, 'The author performs a function, the writer an activity.' He also suggests a division into those who write *something* and those—he calls them the 'real writers'—who do not write something but, rather, *write*. Authors witness to the priority of language, to the performance of the work rather than to the statement of subject matter. They witness to the fulfilment of literature. That is why their preoccupation cannot be with the marketplace, and why it is a mistake to suppose that there is a coherently identifiable community of 'writers' who are like-minded in their commitment to literature.

Paradoxically, none of this is much help in assessing particular books. Hans-Georg Gadamer reminds us that the meaning (the being) of a Text always goes beyond its maker. Some written books transcend their writers, and some authored books fail miserably to be other than routine. Writers sometimes are blind to what is really happening in their work; authors sometimes haven't enough craft skill or the everyday knowledge their books demand. There are times, too, when an author turns writer, usually out of financial need, and yet cannot help but achieve more than is proposed. The best example of this that I know is Alan Garner's *The Stone Book*, which began, by its author's own admission, as an attempt to write the kind of schoolbook his editor had told him was in short supply and ended as one of the finest pieces of children's literature of the period.

Then why bother making the distinction? Because it is there, no matter how difficult to sort out and use critically. Because it has undeniable effects on the production of fiction, and these are worth understanding. Because it again presses the point that readers all too often mistake authorship for manufacturing, looking at pieces of literary sculpture as if they were tables and therefore seeing only failed tables. In the end, I suppose, I'm talking more about readers than about authors. If we could all be authorial-readers who seek for the text written in the book, rather than writer-readers who want only that kind of text we already know about, can easily deal with, and is endlessly repeatable, we would be a nation of literary readers instead of unthinking consumers of one kind of pastime entertainment.

A final word about the network as I've drawn it. There are those who warn against it as inadequate, others who say it is overblown, and some who say it conditions readers into one, rigid view of how the book 'works'. Genette has the answer: 'The "grid" which is so disparaged is not an instrument of incarceration, of bringing to heel, or of pruning that in fact castrates: it is a procedure of discovery, and a way of describing.' If we cannot trust readers to speak for themselves, then there is no hope they will read for themselves either. The incomplete 'discovery' suggested here is simply my own way of trying to sort out what I think I have done. I offer it in the hope that it speaks to your experience of the book.

Inside-Outside

Time forces us on. I could draw a network for *Dance on my Grave* too, but we've had enough of that. Instead, let me tell you how I read *Dance on my Grave* and *Breaktime* as companion novels. They share the same thematic concerns, but approach and treat them differently.

In *Breaktime* all the workings are on show, as all the innards of the Pompidou building in Paris are on show. It is heterosexual, masculine, plain-speaking, revelatory. In *Dance on my Grave* all the workings are hidden, as they are hidden in the walls of, say, a Georgian building, or are inside and under the floorboards. It is homosexual, feminine, ambiguous, aware that nothing ever means only one thing. The reader of *Breaktime* is put into the position of someone standing outside, looking in at the story; the reader of *Dance on my Grave* is looking from the inside out.

Both novels are eclectic in nature; they are collages of different ways of telling: letters, extracts from other fiction, graffiti, newspaper clippings, playscript, concrete verse and prose, cartoons, notebook entries, schoolboy essays, interior monologue, footnotes, impressionist and expressionist modes, lists, parodies—of, for example, B. S. Johnson, Kurt Vonnegut, Laurel and Hardy—and so on, as well as of usual modes of first- and third-person storytelling. Each is placed against the other in order to produce a particular effect and each is chosen because it is the only solution that seemed to satisfy the narrative problem. But in *Breaktime* the ways of telling are offered openly, while in *Dance on my Grave* they are mostly absorbed into the first-person voice of the protagonist, whose writing tends to be as secretive as it is revelatory. Scattered through the book are hidden messages, clues to unstated or coded information, word-game puzzles that are actually serious in intent.

An obvious example is the difference between the two books in treatment of sexual activity. In *Breaktime* Ditto's experiences are explicit; indeed, one of the key scenes in the book, the seduction on the hillside, deals with the question of how you 'tell' about sex so that you communicate its wholeness without being prurient or erotic. In *Dance on my Grave* Hal's experiences with Barry are referred to, you know they're happening, but they're never described. Yet anyone who follows the clues can piece together precisely what is going on.

Dance on my Grave, both in form and content, plays with:

ambiguity: of language, of personality, of motive;

ambivalence: comic and serious, male and female, strong and weak, open and hidden;

symbolic images presented as naturalistic objects and events: the sea, for example, and mirrors, motorbikes, helmets, clothes of one kind and another and what dressing in them means, pictures, gifts. Of the symbolic events one of the most extended and detailed is the long scene with the bikers that begins with Bit 29 and ends with Bit 37 of Part Two. (The raw material for this, by the way, was taken from a maturational dream described and analysed by Carl Jung in *Man and His Symbols*);

ways of telling our experiences. This last is one of the controlling and organizing features in the book's structure. It is, of course, a novel about obsession. Obsession with an image of ideal friendship; obsession with the unsettled meaning of words, and with the unsettling meaning of death; obsession with the way images we fix upon about ourselves compose us—'make us'—into the people we think we are. And above all, obsession with the telling of an experience, that imperative, universally felt desire to put into words what has happened to us.

This 'telling' is in itself a story-within-the-story. My personal conviction is that we are not changed by our experiences, as common wisdom has it. What changes us are the stories we tell about our experiences. Until we have re-formed our lives into story-structured words we cannot find and contemplate the meaning of our lived experiences. Till then they remain in the realm of beastly knowledge. Only by turning the raw material of life into story—by putting it into a pattern of words we call narrative—can beastly knowledge be creatively transformed and given meaning. It is storying that changes us, not events. This conviction lies at the heart of *Dance on my Grave* as Hal writes himself into an understanding of his experience with Barry Gorman.

Hal struggles with the questions: How do I tell about what happened so that it makes sense? How do I tell it so that the telling is true about what happened then but is also true about what is happening now? How is the past turned into the present? How is memory made into meaning? The entire book is a reconsideration through memory; it is about memory and the shifting effects of memory. This being so, each scene must be told as a memory of *then* rediscovered as a reality *now*. (The great sampler, of course, if I could ever finish reading it, is Proust's story of Marcel.)

How to do it? Various narrative solutions are used. Here is an explanation of just one, which provides also an example of what I meant about the author using the writer's craft in the service of his authorial impulse. Television uses this device constantly, especially in sports programmes—that is, during its most action-packed, so-called 'live' shows. The device is Action Replay.

Even as a game of football is in progress, the viewer is shown the action replay of a goal that was scored a few seconds before. The replay will be shown in slow-motion so that we can see whether the goal was offside, say, or a player was fouled or not, even while the referee is still arguing the point with players on the field. And while the slow-motion replay is being shown the unseen presenters give a voice-over commentary in which they remark on the way the goal was scored. That is, they recuperate for us the meaning and significance of the event. They act as a kind of narrator. Of course, if the producer wants to s/he can also use split-screen. Part of the picture will show us the action replay, the other part will show the game as it continues (the referee arguing with the players and then the play starting again). If this is done, we are watching the real present of the game—the game's story as it happens—and the historic present of the goal being scored—the game's immediate past recalled—both at the same time. And when we view these two time-scales together, and simultaneously hear the presenters' discussion of the events, our feelings about the game change, and our view of the real present of the game as it continues changes. We have a different view of the game, and different views about it, from those who are actually there and cannot watch as we watch.

I don't know if all this strikes you with the same force of importance as it strikes me. At any rate, I wanted to use it as a narrative device in order to try to achieve the kind of results in the reader that I believe occur in television viewing of this kind. With the added quality that a novel is a contemplative medium. It allows you time to think, which television, an essentially transient and superficial medium, does not.

Early in *Dance on my Grave* Hal capsizes when sailing single-handed. He is rescued by Barry Gorman, the character who becomes his friend. The scene is central in plot significance; it fixes Hal's state of being at the time, to say nothing of its symbolic implications. Only to have described the capsize would have been to throw all the emphasis on to plot, action, event. To leave contemplative recuperation till later in the story—till, say, that night in bed, when Hal could have remembered it all and thought about it—would have been against the nature of the story itself, and would have delayed the recuperation until after the reader had encountered other events, all of them depending for an understanding of their meaning on the reader's understanding of the meaning of the capsize. Therefore, immediately after the description of the capsize there follows an 'Action Replay' in which Hal's replay in memory is treated linguistically as TV treats such a device visually. You read a slow-motion version with commentary. You contemplate the events even while being told what has happened.

Later on, the device of slow-motion is used again in the scene where Hal is involved in a street brawl. (This is the companion scene to the moment in *Breaktime* when Ditto is hit in the face, which is given the opposite treatment from Hal's: that is, fast-motion shown visually in a cartoon drawing and without commentary.) The focus of the scene is not the fight with the bikers, the what-happens-next, action element of the plot, but the state of being in the fight. For me, the slowing down of the action—the camera angles, so to speak—used to show the events literally blow by blow, the way the slow-motion description allows for commentary which fast-action description hasn't time for, all contribute to making the scene comic and contemplative in nature rather than adventurously exciting in the instant-thrill manner of pulp fiction.

I know I've mentioned contemplation a number of times. That's because, for me, all reading is an act of contemplation. Writing is simply a part of that ritual activity. I write that I may read, and so contemplate that which I have written. Contemplation is important to me because only in contemplation do I realize myself. Some will say that this invests the reading of literature with religious significance. I wouldn't argue with that. For me it has. Perhaps one day I'll write an explanation of its significance. But not yet. For where *Breaktime* and *Dance on my Grave* have led me is to a story about this very idea. I didn't realize they were, of course, while writing them. But I'm amused now to find Hal's teacher, Jim Osborn, telling him, 'If you go on like this you'll turn religious, you know that, don't you?' Sometimes your books know where you're going, or where they're taking you, a long time before you know yourself.

None of my writing, whether fictional or critical, is either an end in itself or ever comes to an end. None of it is self-contained. None of it is finished. All of it belongs, I hope and believe, to a continuum that cannot have an end. Which is as good a note as any on which to end this episode.

Teaching
Children's Literature

This article appeared as a two-part 'Letter from England' in the October and December 1979 issues of *The Horn Book Magazine*.

I

For ten years without a break I have been teaching children's literature to practising teachers from elementary and high schools. Anniversaries make us all incurably retrospective, and I feel a kind of psychological imperative to review the decade of work-in-progress. I cannot say I have arrived at any mind-blowing conclusions. But as the teaching of children's literature to adults and the method of teaching it to children seem on the way to becoming fashionable academic pursuits, we probably all agree about the need to share whatever smidgens of experience we have, even if only to help each other avoid our various mistakes. Hence, I offer you, diffidently, some of my notes to myself.

Before I begin I ought, perhaps, to place my particular experience in context, so that you may make the kind of adjustments-to-circumstance all reported experience needs in order that its value can be assessed. I am, as you know, a full-time author and editor, so my teaching is part-time, usually evening, work. Once a week for about twenty-six weeks a year I meet upwards of twenty to thirty teachers for two-and-a-half-hour sessions. At the end of the course they are examined and walk off, all being well, with a professionally useful extra qualification awarded by the Bristol University School of Education. From time to time I also provide one-day courses as well as five- to ten-week courses primarily intended to help newly interested teachers towards more demanding work. Also, more often than I care to remember, I have been a visiting speaker, giving one-session lectures at other people's seminars and conferences.

Throughout, my basic aims have been the same. I try to help adults build up their knowledge of literature for children while, at the same time, improving their critical understandings, their appreciation of what happens during the act of reading, and their skills in bringing children and books together and in teaching literature to young people.

Now for my notes. Increasingly, to begin with, I'm impressed by a sometimes worrying truth: *Teachers tend to teach in the same way as they were taught and to teach the same books read during their course.* An example still burning my conscience: Only a few weeks ago I led a session in which, at my teachers' request, we talked about poetry and children and looked closely at 'I See a Bear' by Ted Hughes. How, the teachers were asking, do you deal with difficult poetry, and how do you help children into it? The session became a fairly formal exchange between me as tutor and the others as inquiring students. This was not planned; it just happened—my fault for not making sure something more suitable developed. Result: The next day, I learned later, five or six course members went into their schools armed with 'I See a Bear' and, from what I could gather, conducted a precisely similar lesson with their nine- and ten-year-olds.

There was nothing wrong in choosing that poem for their pupils (a good choice, in fact) or in attempting to help children learn how to deal with what only appears to be a difficult piece of writing until you have sorted out how to 'read' it. No, the alarming thing was that they apparently made little attempt to find a mode of language better suited to their pupils' needs than the formal method I had used. Because our session had worked well, they made the assumption that, to achieve the same results with their children, they had to employ exactly the same method as well as the same content.

There is, I suppose, nothing strange or surprising in this. Craftsmen learn technique from one another, and teaching is largely a craft; naturally, when teachers see a colleague doing something effective, they try to emulate it. Unfortunately, part of the craft of teaching is knowing which techniques will work best with particular groups. You can, in fact, teach anything to anybody at any time; but you have to find the methods suited to particular people at any one time.

Nevertheless, the instinctive way in which teachers carry into their work with children the same methods and books with which they were taught means this: *We must look for methods and for literature which unify the teaching of adults and children.* I do not mean that we should never use formal, academic lectures, for example; or that we should carry on with adults as if they were children. Not at all. What this search leads to is a rule-of-thumb I am finding increasingly useful: *Whenever possible put the teacher-student through exactly the same experience as the teacher will ask the child-pupil to go through.*

A simple example: In trying to help children become regular, avid literary readers, many teachers ask their pupils to do two things. Read at least a book a week in their own time; and afterwards write a brief, annotation-like review, giving their opinions of it. There are respectable arguments for this assignment; but it sounds easier to do than it actually is. Therefore, I make it a required part of any course lasting a number of weeks that the teachers do the same thing, not only with children's books (reading these is a professional duty, enjoyable though it may be, and is not part of leisure-time reading) but with a book of adult size.

Usual results: Very soon we discover how hard it is to write annotation-like reviews. That is salutary enough. Better yet, we find out again how hard it is, even with plenty of motivation, to read a substantial piece of literature every week. Furthermore we realize that without the constant presence of a sympathetic person with whom we can talk about what we have read, the whole business can soon become a chore. These experientially reached understandings tell teachers far more about the methods they use than any amount of theoretical discussion can do; and the teachers become much more sensitively aware of the needs of children who are asked to read and report regularly.

Talking about literature—to pick up the last point—and talking about what we thought and felt while reading a book lie at the heart of all teaching of literature. Yet I have to say I find this to be the least well-handled part of all our work in classrooms—whether with adults or with the young.

Two interlinked elements seem to me to determine what happens in our discussions. We bring to the talk a critical stance, our currently favoured view of literature. This predicts the kind of discussion we will generate. If we believe, for example, in the idea that there is one correct reading of a text, we will tend to lead the talk into a kind of right-or-wrong answer, a Socratic dialogue, in which the teacher knows most of the right answers and the pupil tries to give them. This is the game of guessing what is in the teacher's head, and it dominates most Western educational practice. Any pupil whose reading of the text considerably disagrees with the teacher's finds his reading disregarded.

I have written elsewhere about the contract reading makes, which links author, book, and reader. But the fine work of Wolfgang Iser recently brought up to date in his *The Act of Reading* provides the avenues we need to explore in thinking out better and more truly educative teaching strategies than those used in traditional literature teaching.

Principally what we need to develop is the place of the teacher in a literary discussion. S/he must remain a leader, usually one with a far greater experience of literature than the others in the group; but s/he must also behave as just another reader—one among others—all of whom have legitimate and valuable interpretations to offer of any book. As leader, the teacher must help each person discover honestly the book s/he has read; then lead on to discover the book which the author, judged by the narrative's rhetoric, can be agreed upon to have written. And finally, as a result of their corporate and shared experience, the group reconstructs the book they have all read. Thus, the final act is to become aware of the book that comprises each individual interpretation—even the author's—thereby becoming something greater than all.

This is not an act of Socratic cross-examination but of participatory conversation, of exploring and sharing; a creative act, mutually enriching. It is an act of truly democratic proportions, never reductive to a lowest common denominator. On the contrary, when well done, the act elevates the participants to a high mutual achievement and is an example of democratic action in human affairs—as literature is the record of human experience.

Within this act teaching is performed as a contribution of leadership. The teacher offers knowledge of rhetorical devices (the student learns by doing) and must know how to work conversational contributions into some kind of spontaneously organized pattern revealing the underlying movements of the response. In short, the teacher's skill lies in relating articulated responses to the art, craft, and philosophy of literature, so that the student perceives where s/he stands, where others stand, and where the literature is taking her. The teacher raises awareness and is a contributor of specialized knowledge, a guide to further sources, and a synthesizer of disparate and often conflicting comment.

In other words: *Group work in which the teacher-student is a member of a team exploring a literary text or a teaching problem pays high dividends as an educative force and a teaching strategy*. This activity should never be leaderless; on the other hand, the place of leader might often be beneficially given to a student. I have recently been encouraged in such a method by the results of a six-month-long group-work project carried out by nine teachers. Under their own leader they tried to investigate children's responses to literature in order to see what they could learn, especially about how to improve their own teaching. For weeks they appeared to me, as an observing tutor, to be floundering. (The temptation to rush in, take control, and provide direction was all but overwhelming; somehow I resisted.) They read everything they could find about response; they discussed—endlessly, it seemed— what they had read and decided at last to try out one book in all their classrooms: *The Shrinking of Treehorn* by Florence Parry Heide. Gathering together the portable evidence of response—such as artwork, tape recordings, and writing—they linked it with a corporately composed introduction and conclusion.

At the end I asked each teacher to write a five-hundred-word summary about the project. To my pleasure and surprise, there was unanimous agreement about certain aspects, as these typical extracts show:

> The whole activity made me think again about books for children—about the best way to present books, about the expectations a teacher can have in presenting a particular book, and about how best to use the children's response to stimulate further reading and deeper interest in literature.

> The introduction and conclusion were written as a joint effort, which was a laborious and painful experience, but one which we enjoyed. . . . It has also made me think again about group work in the classroom—which I think can be useful if the right sort of conditions are established.

> This group work . . . has changed my attitudes as to how to create the best possible response to the best possible books.

From my point of view as their tutor, what seemed most valuable about the group's work was not so much what they discovered about response or about their own teaching, valuable though this was, but what they learned from the process by which those discoveries were made. The most valuable thing we all learned came from that, not from the content of the project itself.

II

In the early days of my part-time career as a teacher of children's literature, I made the great mistake of ignoring adult literature. Of course, I mentioned certain works in passing. In England, you cannot help nodding at *Lord of the Flies* by William Golding or George Orwell's *Animal Farm*, for instance, because they are so often set for examination study. But it did not occur to me to make connections between the various treatments of childhood and childhood themes in adult literature and those in children's.

I hope I am wiser now. Books like William Trevor's *The Children of Dynmouth* and Susan Hill's *I'm the King of the Castle* add considerably to discussions of the way writers present children in fiction, making clearer by contrast the strengths and weaknesses of children's writers. The opening of John Fowles's *Daniel Martin* presents an extraordinary parallel to *The Aimer Gate*, the third volume of Alan Garner's *Stone Book* quartet.

Then there are questions of narrative technique. A bit of reading in B. S. Johnson, James Joyce, Donald Barthelme, and Kurt Vonnegut, Jr, helps, if nothing else, to show the considerable technical limitations of many children's authors, and the considerable skill of a few.

These days, one of those guiding ideas which form my courses is: *Every teacher-student shall be required to include in his/her reading a proportion of adult literature.* During the course we discuss new books and deliberately set out to match various children's and adult works. But this is not done solely because there may be stimulating connections between the two. More importantly, it is done because neglect of mainstream literature can only lead to an insufficiently informed understanding of children's literature. It will lack the context of its literary culture. People who read only children's books have noticeably distorted perspectives. They tend to overvalue routine writing and misunderstand significantly innovative work— like *The Stone Book* quartet and *Fungus the Bogeyman* by Raymond Briggs, a modern novel in comic-strip disguise.

In the end, literature must be seen as a whole, not as something contained in watertight compartments. In fact, literature is composed of individual books, and—at best—all of them should be available to all of us all the time. Certainly, in my experience the people who have the most interesting things to say about children's literature are also those who read and think about adult literature. And having seen the benefits of encouraging teachers to read widely in both, I'm quite sure that children's literature courses which ignore such broadening and deepening work will lack a significant element.

To some extent the same is true if students of children's literature are not given the opportunity and encouragement to write their own children's stories, poems, and plays. By doing this they discover from the author's side—practically rather than theoretically and critically—the pressing artistic and technical problems that face a writer for the young. Such understanding helps critical and pedagogic activity: We get to know more about what literary problems to look for and how to assess an individual author's solutions of them; and we appreciate in a different way the needs of literature itself when we are bringing it to children. But particular books need particular kinds of treatment when we are helping others to read them, and a good teacher will know this and be able to sort out what those needs are.

The important thing about writing stories is the act itself, not any thought of publication. We are not trying to make teacher-students into authors but simply trying to help them discover the author's problems. And we are suggesting to them that a sufficiently sustained attempt at literary writing for children inevitably makes one a more consciously skilled reader of children's literature and a more sympathetic teacher: sympathetic as much to the books as to the children.

Because my tutoring work is part-time and lacks a permanent base, I must meet my teachers in whatever building is allotted to me. More often than not, this means a room devoid of everything a reader needs—which has taught me another lesson similar to the one I outlined earlier. Just as teachers tend to teach in the same way they were taught and tend to use the same books with their children as were used with them, so teachers tend to create the same kind of reading environment as the one they were taught in.

Therefore, ideally—and I have been totally defeated in achieving this for myself—*we should work in rooms and in conditions exactly like those we know children need if they are to become readers.* That is, there should be a large and very wide-ranging selection of literature in sight and easily available. The books should be shelved and displayed in attractive and intelligently enticing ways. There should be literature-related artefacts: posters; samples of printers' hardware; children's and adults' response work, such as paintings, models, writings. It should be easy to find comfortable places to sit and read or write.

An early part of the course should be devoted to the reading environment, in which all the elements should be described and discussed—the things I've already mentioned as well as such topics as browsing time, time to read, and reading aloud. During the rest of the course individual teachers should be supported in their efforts to create an ideal reading environment in their own schools.

Which leads me to my last point for now. What ten years of teaching children's literature has taught me most clearly is that, so far as children and literature are concerned, the literature itself and critical approaches to it cannot be divorced from considerations of how the literature should be mediated to children. Put another way: *Any comprehensively useful criticism of children's literature must incorporate a critical exploration of the questions raised by the problem of helping children to read the literature.*

Indeed, the study of the act of reading itself is essential for anyone involved in children and books. Naturally, therefore, in a recent five-week tour of the U.S.A. I was distressed to find that in your country as in mine the study of literature, the study of the act of reading, and the study of children's literature are not seen as one study but as three—and three studies that need never be brought together.

In the next few years, when children's literature will be institutionalized by professional academics, it will be a serious misfortune for us all if these three totally interrelated aspects of our field are kept apart. This is why in my own small teaching activity I now design my one-year courses so that they always include these features:

1. A ground-base of reading as the main element. This comprises a foundation of children's literature; a proportion, next in importance, of adult literature; and a few key critical texts to do with rhetorical criticism and the phenomenology of reading.

2. Each teacher-student must keep a briefly annotated record of what s/he reads, both professionally and privately.

3. Everyone is required to write a feature piece—a conventional

123

critically directed study of a book, an author, or a collection of books. And everyone is encouraged to attempt a story, poem, or play for children, which is then used as raw material for discussion of narrative problems.

4. Seminar and group-organized explorations of three broad topics: the act of reading as a phenomenological event; the act of criticism as a rhetorical study; and the act of mediating literature to children as a pedagogic-critical performance. These three topics are interwoven and presented as facets of the same specialist discipline.

I wonder whether in another ten years I will have revised all this apparently clear-cut certainty and look back on it with as much amusement at its inadequacy as I presently look back at the beginnings of my work ten years ago.

Whose
Book is it Anyway?

This is the third of three papers I was asked to give at the Conference of the Australian branch of the International Board on Books for Young People held at the University of Sydney in August 1983. The conference theme title was 'Changing Faces: Story and Children in an Electronic Age'; other contributors talked about such matters as television and computers in relation to children's reading. This paper was given at the last session of the conference, and is included here because it says something about our developing understanding of the relationship between modern critical theory and work with children, and because it makes a useful introduction to the article, 'Tell Me: Are Children Critics?'

*

At the close of our conference I'd like to talk about error, forgetfulness, and boredom. Along the way I'll dwell on playfulness, fracture and puzzlement. If I have time, I'll finish with linkage, and with a few comments about people on the make. In other words, I'd like to talk about the end of reading.

It seems to me that reading is a three-act drama. Act One is about selection: choosing what to read, where to read it, when to read it. Act Two is about reading what we have chosen to read, and is a performance that requires us to be withdrawn, book-absorbed, even anti-social for considerable periods of time. Act Three is about reconstruction.

It is about Act Three that I want to talk. Sometimes this third act masquerades as a separate drama in its own right. Then, considerable attention is paid to those performing it. Often, they receive more rewards in honours, money, and status than the people who actually wrote the scripts on which the entire drama is based. When this happens, when Act Three is made into a play of its own, we call it criticism. When it is not so elevated, or of course when we want to condescend to the people we observe doing it, we simply call it response. That's why, in order to avoid misrepresentation, I've decided to call Act Three: Reconstruction. By which I mean: re-making, re-forming, re-structuring. And the way I'd like to talk about Act Three is to tell you a few short stories about children performing some acts of reconstruction.

The first story is called 'The Tale of the High School Levellers'. The setting is a school in an English town; the characters are a group of about eight students of both sexes, aged seventeen. They are just starting the first term of a six-term, two-year course leading to university-qualifying A-level examinations in English literature. Their expectation is that they will arrive for their first lesson and begin at once the study of set texts, such as Shakespeare's *King Lear*, perhaps Thomas Hardy's *The Mayor of Casterbridge*, and maybe the poetry of Ted Hughes.

Instead, their teacher, a lively young woman, lays before them a collection of about twenty children's picture books, including such standards as Pat Hutchins's *Rosie's Walk* at one extreme and Raymond Briggs's *Fungus the Bogeyman* at the other. She tells them to look at the books, read them, talk about them; if they like, they may jot down notes about things they might want to mention in discussion later. But all they have to do is notice their thoughts, feelings, memories, as they read.

The immediate reaction is of shock-horror. What can their teacher be thinking of, making them attend to baby books, when she should be instructing them in the examination-passing secrets of Shakespeare, Hardy and Hughes? She asks them to trust her, get on with the job, and promises they will very soon discover for themselves the link between picture books and examination passes in Shakespeare. During that first lesson shock-horror turns to shock-surprise, and the group's absorbed fascination is evident in their enthusiasm for the books. Now, apparently, picture books are not for children; they are far too complicated. The ways in which they are complicated are pointed out. Student after student reports subtle interweavings of words and pictures, varieties of meanings suggested but never stated, visual and verbal clues to intricate patterns, structures, ideas.

Lesson after lesson in their first week the reading continues. Particular books are fastened on to. Anthony Browne's treatment of

Hansel and Gretel becomes required reading for everyone, provoking considerable agreement, disagreement, and argument about the 'rightness' of different interpretations, and of Browne's pictures. Sendak's *Outside Over There*, which also becomes required reading, is said by one student to be entirely unsuitable for children, apparently because it maintains a disturbing sexual stance. (The teacher smiles to herself as she hears all the old adult arguments being noised again in her classroom as if they were bold new insights.)

The class quickly cottons on to the fact that every one of the books, no matter how simple it appears at first sight, contains within it a multiplicity of possible readings, and that, as Frank Kermode puts it in his *Essays on Fiction 1971–82*, 'the illusion of the single right reading is possible no longer' [p. 102]. Even in *Rosie's Walk*, they realize, there is no possibility of a single right reading that suggests whether Rosie knew all the time that the fox was behind her, or that she didn't. And who is the joke about, the hen or the fox? The possibility is easily understood—it can be seen in the pictures—that, within the fiction, by the way form controls content, both readings are not only possible at the same time, but are necessary.

And so this group of seventeen-year-olds discovered rapidly, by their return to the very books which, in some cases, are the ones that best help four- and five-year-olds learn to read, that criticism is not about error, not about being right or wrong, that there never can be a definitive reading, but only additional readings, all of them in some way revealing, on the one hand of the reader him/herself, and on the other hand of the patterns contained within the mythos we call a Text.

Because of this experience the teacher could later say that this was the first class she had started on A-level work which did not struggle with the question, 'How do you know Shakespeare meant all these things people say he meant?', but began instead to look at once for the multiple readings offered in the patterns of language presented by the writing. They had learned, by performance rather than instruction, a truth summarized by Jonathan Culler, out of Jacques Derrida, in his book *On Deconstruction*:

There is nothing that might not be put into a literary work; there is no pattern or mode of determination that might not be found there. To read a text . . . as literature is to remain attentive even to its apparently trivial features. A literary analysis is one that does not foreclose possibilities of structure and meaning in the name of the rules of some limited discursive practice. [p. 182]

Most of all they learned by reconstructing for themselves what Barthes tells us about the birth of the reader being at the cost of the death of the author; or, as Hans-Georg Gadamer writes, 'Not occasionally only, but always, the meaning of a text goes beyond its author'. [*Truth and Method*, p. 264]

'The Tale of the High School Levellers' does not end here. Theirs was one of the most stimulating reading-and-teaching projects I've observed and suggests what creative encounters schools and universities can offer students if their professors and tutors give themselves, in their teaching, to the ideas they expound so often in their discussion of literary theory.

The second story for today is 'The Case of the Boy Who Forgot'. This is a very short story and, forgive me, involves one of my own books. Before I left home to visit you I spent a day in a primary school where some of the ten-year-olds had helped me with background material for *The Present Takers*. (I needed to know such essential information as: What do girls of ten carry in their school bags? Which words are the most wounding when a girl bully uses them? On such matters does conviction hang!) My helpers had read pre-publication copies of the book, and I was to hear their comments. During one of the sessions with a class who had had the story read aloud to them, a boy, Robert, asked: 'At the end, why doesn't Melanie Prosser [the bully] blackmail Lucy [the protagonist] with the notes sent her by Angus [Lucy's would-be helpmate] instead of letting Lucy and Angus get the better of her?' Before I could reply there were shouts of 'Because Melanie hasn't got the notes, stupid! She gave them back to Lucy, and Lucy dropped them in the gutter, remember?'

Robert blushed, then claimed he must have been absent when that bit was read, and then said, 'Well, I remember now.' There followed a discussion about Angus's notes, about sending messages illicitly in class, about blackmail, about why Lucy dropped the notes into the gutter, about the final breakdown of the bully in the face of concerted, passive, but public witness by the victims of her malignity, and finally about why and how writing is different from talking. Robert's forgetfulness had, in fact, led us to the heart of the book, had involved us in explorations of the story in a way we might not otherwise have done. His forgetfulness had provoked and focused critical discussion. Besides this, his question had proposed a possible alternative pattern of plot, an alternative 'What if . . .?' that would have upset the thematic network of the book had it been followed; would, I mean, have produced a different narrative outcome. Trying that out could have helped us understand the author's version.

All this will be obvious to you. But consider what usually happens; what indeed is partly evidenced in this story. When Robert asked his question, thus unwittingly revealing his forgetfulness, he was treated with scorn by the rest of the class at once and instinctively. Robert blushed at what he must have thought of as his mistake, tried to dodge his way out by suggesting an excuse (that he'd been absent), and then tried to regain the initiative by asserting that, after all, he remembered, as if regaining a memory of information would redeem him in the eyes of his peers. In other words, he finally and successfully excused himself by remembering. He might equally well have been dodging with this answer too, he might actually have been absent and only pretending to remember, because claiming to remember after making an error of information was more meritorious than never having heard the information in the first place. Better to have known, forgotten, and then remembered, than never to have known at all.

If this chimes with your experience, join me in asking why this should be so. Two points. First, our educational system places such value on remembering as a test of cleverness and character that to forget is regarded as a weakness, and to remember more worthy than not to know. People will, and constantly do, lie about knowing something they have never heard of before. Microelectronic machines, by the way, being in part simply memory banks engineered so as to provide recall faster than anyone can manage for themselves, will change our attitude to fact-memory, making those with poor recall equal in status with those who are better endowed.

The second point. In reading literature forgetfulness is vital. Our minds use forgetfulness to push aside elements of a text that mean too much for us just then, or to separate out and emphasize those elements that we are most ready to deal with. Robert's question was a hinge. His mind used it to turn him from 'pushing away' the meanings to do with retribution and bring them now to his attention. Remembrance, after all, is the companion of forgetfulness. Besides, if we could remember everything in a story all the time, how soon it would seem exhausted, how quickly it would seem worn out, finished, lifeless. In reading—during the performance and in thoughtful reconstruction afterwards—the Text is always *becoming*. It is never finally 'made'. 'Forgetting meanings,' Barthes tells us in *S/Z*, 'is not a matter for excuses, an unfortunate defect in performance; it is an affirmative value, a way of asserting the irresponsibility of the text, the pluralism of systems.' He adds, 'It is precisely because I forget that I read.' [p. 11]

In both stories, 'The Tale of the High School Levellers' and 'The Case of the Boy Who Forgot', something else was going on than those features I've so far pointed out. In each, readers were describing what had happened to them as they read. They were telling the story of their reading. The A-level students even talked their stories aloud like simultaneous commentaries as they looked at picture books. Robert, though unwittingly, told about a time after reading, the moment when he forgot.

My third story is also an example of what happens when we quite openly tell about our reading, and it is called 'The Boy Who was Bored'.

One rather warm afternoon—maybe the heat had something to do with it—I was working with another teacher and a class of fifteen-year-olds. My colleague had insisted that our pupils write review reports on their set books. (You can see how long ago this was; I was still a schoolteacher and youngish in my profession; I would never countenance such a method now.) A boy called Stephen submitted a report composed of only one sentence: 'This is the most boring book I have ever read.' My colleague glared at it, became extremely angry, roundly abused Stephen for impudence, insubordination, and the rest of the insults teachers at their worst can throw at children unchallenged, and then ordered him from the room. This was, of course, a failure of relationship, of duty and of discipline. Much worse, however, it was a failure of understanding on the part of the teacher. He plainly did not know what reading and critical reconstruction involve. Boredom in reading is not only to be expected but is, like forgetfulness, inescapable. Boredom is part of being a reader. Just as it is part of the reconstructive act for readers *to say*—to speak out the experiences, including the experience of boredom, that happen during their reading.

Thus one of the most useful and stimulating questions anyone can ask a group of readers is this: Tell me about the parts of the story that bored you. For what has happened when we grow bored? We are reading along, deep in pleasure, wanting more. We find suddenly, or perhaps gradually over a page or two, that we are no longer deep in pleasure, but have 'surfaced'. We are now easily distracted. Why? Because our energies have run out? This would be a reason to do with our personal, extra-book life. But, just like our extra-book life, our intra-book life also has a rhythm. And if we look again at what we have just read we might find, for example, that the story's structure has made a shift. There is a new tune to attend to, or a development of an earlier tune has taken over, or in some other way the story has changed. Our minds, however, linger still on the passage just finished. We're still attached to it, still want to live in it. This new passage is a disturbance, an interruption, against which we protect ourselves by a withdrawal of attention, by, as we say, becoming bored.

Of course, during another reading, the very passage we found so boring before can now rivet our attention, penetrating us so deeply that we feel the same excitement and absorbed attention that we experienced with the earlier passage. This is also, surely, our common experience of reading? And is equally surely the reason for rereading? We desire not simply to re-experience the first rapture, but to discover quite different sites, different contexts, for renewed rapture. Intercourse with a book is a promiscuous and insatiable appetite, always wanting the new, the surprising. If a book proves too prim, ungiving of any but the same story each time, then we dismiss it and do not return again and again. Every work of literature wants to be, within itself, a Scheherazade.

This analysis is crude, not taking into account an infinite number of possibilities, extra-book and intra-book, that can cause boredom. All I want to say here is that boredom is a fact of our reading lives and has such importance that we should attend to it in our work with young and inexperienced readers. So what should have been done with the boy who was bored? His report should have been used as the start of a discussion. The pattern of his boredom should have been explored. People take as much pleasure in telling what they disliked as what they liked. And they as often disagree about the passages that bored them most as about those they enjoyed. The resulting reconstruction creates the kind of comparative discussion of a work and its Text that leads to greater understanding, and the production of greater pleasure. This sharing is itself a rereading that constructs a newly ordered Text, a book that might otherwise never have been discovered: the book that we make together.

What goes on in all critical/responsive talk is that we share our enthusiasms, share our puzzlements, and share the connections of meaning encountered between the book and ourselves—first ourselves individually and then ourselves communally. For by sharing the Texts we each individually hold within us—a different book for each one, though we have all read the same book—we build another, corporate and multiple Text, always more complex, always more interesting, always other than the Text we made our own as we read. And we achieve this simply by telling the story of our own reading and listening to the stories others tell of their reading.

Jonathan Culler puts it this way: 'An interpretation of a work thus comes to be an account of what happens to the reader: how various conventions and expectations are brought into play, where particular connections or hypotheses are posited, how expectations are defeated or confirmed.' [p. 35] Of course the most impressive and critically sophisticated example of this is to be found in Roland Barthes' *S/Z*. But children, even very young children, can do it, if a sympathetic adult who understands the process leads the way. [As my article 'Tell Me: Are Children Critics?' on page 138 tries to show.] Always, *always*, the adults who stand between children and books make us into the kind of readers we become. The adults who do this best put before children all kinds of story—all sorts of form and content—and help children tell the story of their reading, help them discover for themselves the potency and variety of literature.

Stephen, the boy who was bored, could have enlivened a classroom discussion otherwise dominated by pupils who were too keen to say what was expected of them. His explanation of his boredom might have released others from the bonds of their conditioning, which had taught them that they must pretend to possess responses that were not their own. Better yet, he might have taught himself that what happened to him as he read, *whatever* that might be, was not only a fact of his life, but was honourably and usefully reportable. For this was the raw material that could have fed his pleasure in reading and helped his understanding of literature, and of himself, to grow. As it was, his treatment merely confirmed to himself and everyone else that literature was not about *them*, but was about what unknown and apparently superior beings told them it was about, and then required them to repeat as if they themselves, the pupils, had honestly thought it. No teaching could be more dishonest, more productive of a cynical and disaffected community. The result is total and non-literary boredom of a kind that rejects the printed literature of their mother tongue by the majority of our people.

This is not, however, a state of affairs that is irredeemable. I have seen, as must many of you, a change in such bad teaching practice happen within a year, and a whole school recover its literary pride, its excitement in reading. What a school can do a nation can do. Which brings me to the story of 'The Children who played I Spy'.

A new head teacher in an English primary school was concerned about the routine dullness of her school's literary life. She began seeing her children in groups of six or seven, a couple of groups every afternoon. All she did was show them some books, read to them, let them talk informally about what they'd read, and listen to what they said to each other. One of the books she showed them was Anthony Browne's *A Walk in the Park*. She was surprised to find that these children of eight and nine were noticing things she had not noticed herself, though she thought she knew the book well, and that their reasons for the pictorial oddities were often surprising and, even more, were also extraordinarily suggestive of possible meanings. From that base she went on to revise her school's approach to literature, turning it into a lively reading environment. [I have described this experience in 'Axes for Frozen Seas' on page 26, so I won't repeat the detail here.]

To a passing observer, the children poring over *A Walk in the Park* might have seemed to be doing nothing but playing. Well, much has been said by recent critical theorists about the ludic—about playfulness—in literature, a vast amount of which speaks importantly to children's literature, its writers, teachers, adult readers. (I have often wondered why literary theorists haven't yet realized that the best demonstration of almost all they say when they talk about phenomenology or structuralism or deconstruction or any other critical approach can be most clearly and easily demonstrated in children's literature. The converse of which is to wonder why those of us who attend to children's literature are, or have been, so slow in drawing the two together ourselves.) But what is deep in the nature of play? Apart, I mean, from the usual wisdom about it as a way of learning. What I have in mind is this. Playfulness, especially game-playfulness, is about exhaustion. In a game we try to exhaust all the possibilities. We try to find the answers, win the points, leave our partner bereft. A game is over when everything has been achieved or acquired; play finishes when the rules are completed, or everyone has had a turn, or when the script—to move the metaphor into the play of theatre—has been said and acted. Nothing remains but the experience of having done it—or rather, what remains is the memory of the experience.

The ludic in literature is finally about the exhaustion of language. Authors try to complete language, make an end of it, use it all. Each book, when it is published, is a dissatisfaction to its author because it does not do what s/he set out to do: finish with language. So another book has to be written in the—what?—foolish, mad?—no: in the neurotically obsessive desire to achieve linguistic repletion. As for readers, they always want to get to the end, want to finish the book. Have you seen how naïve adolescent readers reach for the shortest book, look to see how much type is on the page and choose the one with the least? Is it not ironic that when choosing something to read they should choose that which has in it the least to read? I guess all of us hope that one day we will discover a short wonderful book that exhausts the language in one brief, all-consuming flourish, a final excruciating orgasm of pleasure ending in death!

We know we won't of course, which is why we reread those books that come nearest to doing so. We think that this time through we'll discover the hidden book, the one we missed last time, and there, then, it will be over. Even so, we also know we cannot exhaust language. We know that language exhausts us. Language transcends people, that's the truth of it. But we go on trying to be the masters, the ones in control, by again and again setting out as if we can finish language, and always end up with it finishing us. That is the real game, the ludic quality in reading.

One of the things that sometimes bothers me is the lack of sufficiently ludic richness in many children's books. Too many of them are plain, unnecessarily limited. I can show why this sometimes happens. Remember the story of 'The Boy who Forgot'? When I asked the two groups of children which parts of *The Present Takers* they enjoyed most, the answer was the same both from those who had heard the story read aloud and from those who had read it privately for themselves. It was a passage they called 'the row in Woolworth's'. This turned out not to be a whole scene but a moment when the three central characters shout at each other all at once. On the page the dialogue is presented in three parallel columns, one for each charac-ter, and each line matching word for word the simultaneity of the characters' dialogue, until Lucy alone shouts the word 'steal', which ends the row.

The group who had heard the book read aloud liked this best, apparently, because their teacher, when she reached this point, showed them the page in order to explain why she couldn't read it, then brought out two children, and together they enacted the shouted passage, each taking a part as in a play. This shift from read-aloud to theatre clearly gave considerable pleasure. But more: they then began talking about what had happened to them as they listened. Some, they found, had 'heard' one of the characters dominantly, some another. Not everyone had listened to the same voice. And no one could listen to all three at once. To sort out all that had been said and meant in the row, they had to reconstruct their different experiences as listeners and pool them. Simply by its narrative form the book had forced them into playing the third act of the reading drama—the act of reconstruction—even while they were still engaged in the second act—the performance of reading. The readers at this point had become the writer. They were making the story and its meaning together.

The children in the second group, the private readers, also agreed, quite independently, that this was one of the most enjoyable parts. But in their case the visual effect of the three columns of type had especially interested them, and then they chose which column to read first, second and third. They differed (this was their surprise discovery as they told me about it) in the order they had chosen. They had not all read from the left-hand column through to the right-hand column, as I had expected they would. But, of course, they had all had to pause in the steady flow of their reading. The narrative had been 'held up'. Yet rather than diminish their pleasure, this interruption had increased it. They had been absorbed by the game, while at the same time being made to stand back from the narrative action and consider what it meant. They had had to perform an act of reconstruction while still making an originating act of construction. So they experienced the pleasures of immediacy and involvement at the same time as the pleasures of thoughtful, distanced criticism. (This is quite a different event, by the way, from the arbitrary interruption of a narrative by a teacher who wants to check that pupils are listening or have understood the story so far, and asks them questions about what is going on. In the experience I'm recounting the story itself caused the interruption of the narrative flow, but maintained concentration on the narrative. The hold-up was itself part of the story.)

They enjoyed this because form and content combined attractively. But while writing the story I wondered whether ten- and eleven-year-old readers would find this moment offputting. Also, my editor discussed it with me, wondering the same thing. Only my experience observing such events as 'The Children who played I Spy' made me confident that the story worked best that way and that children would read the passage not only without difficulty but with increased enjoyment. Even if they wouldn't have done years ago, they do now because film and television have made such narrative strategies commonplace.

Yet still we hear that children require and like best stories that work in a steady, consistent, and uninterrupted flow of narrative manner and event, and that 'fractured narrative', as it is sometimes mistakenly called, is either disliked or beyond them. My experience as author, reader, teacher, is quite contrary to this. Richness, density, an amenable surface with much complexity to be found below: that is the kind of literature that appeals to me and to many children also. Of course it does so only if there is linkage. All stories are made out of other stories; all our reading is made by the stories we've read. If we are shown only a narrow range of literature, then we become readers of that restricted kind of writing.

If you want to get rich as a reader you need to go prospecting in a country rich in ores. Whether you mess about with a rock hammer and pan, or whether you move in with big equipment and all the training you can get, readers are, when they are properly literary, always on the make. They want a payoff, and they want thick lodes that aren't buried too deep to dig for. Single-person outfits or international combines, what they all do is buy up the country, take it over and make it their own till they've exhausted it. Then they leave for new and unexploited places. If the lode is rich enough, they settle down, build their homes, pretty the place up, show people around, and start talking about conservation.

It's like that with literature. Except that literature is the richest lode of the lot. And it's alive. You can't exhaust it because it is self-generating. Cut out some and more appears. And it's better than gold because everybody can own the same bit at the same time. The microelectronic book we have been speculating about, will, we hope, provide us with a way of writing, and with a reading machine that will put more of the lode into more people's hands. So whose book is it? Yours, mine, ours: everybody's who has become a reader. Every book belongs to those who make up the community of its readers.

Tell Me:
Are Children Critics?

with Irene Suter, Barbara Raven, Jan Maxwell

Anna Collins and Steve Bicknell

Recently Steve Bicknell, a teacher colleague and friend, began a letter to me:

> It's strange how the opinions of young children echo our own. At our last meeting you said, 'The act of reading lies in talking about what you have read.' Looking back through my notes of conversations I've participated in with children, I constantly return to a remark by eight-year-old Sarah (not usually noted for her willingness to risk an opinion in front of her class): 'We don't know what we think about a book until we've talked about it.'

Steve is one of six of us who meet regularly every three weeks. We discuss literature, children, and teaching, and help each other understand better what we try to do in our work. Steve is deputy head in a Swindon, Wiltshire, junior school. The others, all presently primary teachers, are: Irene Suter, a head; Jan Maxwell, a deputy head; Anna Collins and Barbara Raven, both senior members of their school staffs; and myself, a full-time writer, ex-full-time teacher, and sometimes an in-service tutor of courses the others took part in several years ago, when we first met. In age we range from the early thirties to the mid fifties, in experience from rural to inner-city schools and from infant to secondary school sixth-form. For one reason and another the full-time five have all settled in primary schools; I am in and out of all kinds of classroom as visiting author, and am presently tutoring student teachers.

Over the years we have helped each other acquire a reasonably sound knowledge of contemporary children's books, have examined closely and done something about the school as a 'reading environment' (a term we coined in our early encounters years ago), and have explored reading methods that bring children and literature together. All along, given the pressure of our working days, we have thought that we should keep ourselves in touch as best we can with critical theory and practice. Recently we have attended particularly to this last aspect of our agenda, finding in the exploration of the phenomenology of reading (Iser) and in structuralism (Barthes especially) lines of thought useful in our teaching of children.

Years ago I drew the diagram of 'The Reading Circle' (described in detail in *Introducing Books to Children* and summarized here on page 11), which helped us tackle any espisode in the act of reading without losing touch with the other episodes in the drama. If we were talking about book selection, for example, the Reading Circle reminded us to consider each book in relation to the books our children had read before and its demands if it is to be 'read' with understanding. I put quote marks round that word 'read' because we learned that 'reading' is not one process concerned only with that time when words on a page are being scanned, but is a dramatic performance composed of many related scenes. Helping children engage in the drama of reading, helping them become dramatist, director, performer, audience, even critic, was how we sometimes told ourselves about our work.

As we looked more and more closely at the Circle we realized it was a map drawn by people who thought the reading world was flat. This is how we said it: Suppose a child, as many do, selects a story by Enid Blyton, settles down and 'reads' it, enjoys it so much that s/he goes to the shelves and finds another by the same author, 'reads' it, finds another, and so on. According to our map we were observing a 'reading child'. But of course we were uneasy. Repetitious reading of any kind of book, of any one author, is flat-earth reading. It may not know about, or worse still may not acknowledge, that the world is round, plural, disparate, many-faceted. Flat-earthers resist any invitation to explore beyond the boundaries of their familiar territory because of the fearsome dangers they are sure lie in wait at the edge of their world. One of these dangers is called boredom, another is called difficulty. A third is fear of exhaustion (perhaps the journey round the other side—if there is another side!—will never end). There are many more well known to teachers:

139

'I couldn't get past the first page/chapter.'

'It wasn't my kind of book.'

'It looks long. I'll never get through it.'

'I don't like the cover/title/author/blurb/hardbacks/paperbacks/ print/paper/smell.'

'There aren't any pictures.' (Shades of Alice!)

'There's a lot of hard words.'

Et cetera.

What was it, we asked ourselves, that changed people from being flat-earth readers into not just round-earth but intergalactic readers? How do we turn a closed circle into a rising spiral?

In seeking answers to earlier questions, we had learned to ask them about ourselves. We did the same here. We regard ourselves as fairly typical of the people we teach. We were all brought up in conventional working-class and lower-middle-class homes, attended neighbourhood schools, met with the variety of competence and incompetence there to be found. Some of us were 'late developers' in reading, others were avid book devotees from infancy. Some of us had been flat-earth readers and had changed. Why had our reading 'taken off'? What keeps it spiralling even now?

We found some answers quickly. We had all been deeply affected as children, and still were, by what others, whom we liked, respected, and would *listen to*, said about books they had read and which we then read because of them. We had all been affected, and still were, by what we *found ourselves* saying during conversations about books we'd read. It was in what other people told us about their reading, and what we told of our own, that we thought we had discovered the heart of the matter. It was booktalk that pumped blood into our literary veins and gave us the energy, the impetus, for exploration beyond our familiar boundaries. We could all recount vivid memories of people who were particularly important in our lives for this reason, some of whom were teachers. We could all recall moments of booktalk that sent our lives another turn up the literary spiral.

But not all talk, and not everybody's talk, worked like that. Were there, we wondered, certain kinds of talk, were there features in it, that were most effective? Could we isolate those features, even codify them perhaps? Could they at least be learned and used in our talk with children? We began taking apart booktalk in the hope of finding out how it worked. We considered theories of reading and of reader response. We looked at what we knew of critical theory and practice, hoping this might help. Constantly we came back to ourselves and our own talk and tried to untangle what went on in it.

The more we did the more we became convinced of the essential part talk plays in even the most sophisticated reader's reading life, never mind the centrally important part it plays in learning-children's lives. That was why at one of our recent meetings I said with such apparently unqualified conviction the line Steve quoted back at me in his end-of-year letter: 'The act of reading lies in talking about what you have read.'

We know this will seem obvious to most people. We thought so ourselves as we said it. I repeat it because we need to establish the ground we are working over, but also for a more important reason. It isn't so much the talk but the nature of the talk that matters. And it was this, the nature of the discourse, that we soon realized we must concentrate on. The rest of this article tells some of the things we thought and did. It records the 'levels of talk' we sorted out to help our teaching. It takes samples of children's talk and explores what they seem to be saying. It re-examines the question shockingly put one evening by Rene Suter at the end of a long session during which we had become excited by the self-teaching power of some of our children's talk: 'In that case,' Rene asked, 'could someone tell me what we think the teacher *does*?' Most importantly, it offers for your scrutiny the aid we came to call 'The Framework', a question-posing guide we use in our booktalk with ourselves and our children in an effort to enable us all in becoming critically appreciative (galactic) readers.

Finally by way of introduction I should emphasize that this is not a report of 'research' in the generally understood sense, but is an account of six teachers finding their way by largely pragmatic methods towards a greater craft skill in their work. It is as a piece of correspondence, a letter to friends, rather than as an essay that we would like it to be read.

Levels of Saying

When we examined our own and our children's talk about books we rediscovered those familiar categories presented, for example, in the Dartmouth Report and re-expressed in my grouping suggested in *Introducing Books to Children* as 'The Three Sharings': the sharing of enthusiasms, the sharing of puzzles, and the sharing of connections. But we also could discern a different set of functions, each having a private and a public effect, and which we called 'The Four Levels of Saying':

1. *Saying for Yourself*   The private motivation for this speech act is the need to hear said what we have so far only inwardly thought, because, as is so often repeated, 'we don't know what we think till we hear what we say.' But saying out loud demands a listener. We need someone prepared to hear what we're saying because this somehow alters our own perception of what we are saying. The entrance of a listener, however, means the act has a public effect. It draws others into the activity of clarifying our own minds, and leads both sayer and listener, therefore, naturally to the second 'level'.

2. *Saying for Others*   Whether we speak in order to clarify our own minds, or in order to communicate our thoughts to another person (or, more likely, in hope of doing both at once), the saying of a thought to someone else means that the listener has now thought it too. At this second level, then, the private motivation is to communicate with others, and the public effect is to make our thoughts into corporately owned possessions. By owning the thoughts of others we each extend the range of our ability to think and the limits of our individual potential by the addition of the range of the other speakers in the group. In short, we each take on the power of the others' thoughts.

Steve Bicknell provides this example of the second level from a lesson with his eight-year-olds.

We were talking about Sendak's *Where the Wild Things Are* and things weren't particularly interesting. Nobody had mentioned dreams or imagination; we were still busy with likes and dislikes. To move things on I asked them to tell me about what they didn't understand. Several immediately began comparing illustrations and saying how they couldn't understand how trees would grow in Max's room. I said, 'Yes, that's certainly a bit strange.' Wayne replied, 'He's having a dream.' Several 'Oh, yeah's followed and some looked even more confused. I asked for a show of hands. 'Who agrees with Wayne?' The majority agreed and claimed they had always known it to be a dream! Wayne had actually, I think, enabled the others to possess what he had said and, also, by saying it had made others convinced that they had already thought it.

3. *Saying Together*   The private motivation here is to sort out with

other people matters too difficult and complex for us to sort out alone. The public effect of the application of our pooled powers of thought is that we reach a 'reading'—a knowledge, understanding and appreciation of a book—that far exceeds what any one member of the group could possibly have achieved alone. Corporate reading is always a fissionable drama.

4. *Saying the New*   The private motivation here is the desire to engage in booktalk for the sake of the activity and its results in themselves. (Once known never forgotten and ever after wished for.) The most profound and attractive nature of this experience is the discovery during talk of new thoughts no one till that moment had known or could have said. Saying thoughts together creates new thoughts that lie beyond us all. The sensation is of 'lift off', of flight into the hitherto unknown. It is the experience of revelation. By close attention *together* the text begins to reward us with riches we did not know it possessed.

The public effect of so productive an experience is that people come to know by lively understanding the social importance of literary reading. They perceive at first hand how it transcends pastime entertainment, bedtime cosiness, or everyday functional value. How, rather, it offers us images to think with and a means of creating and re-creating the very essence of our individual and corporate lives.

Having distinguished between these 'sayings' we soon realized they suggest questions that could guide our teaching:

1. *Saying for Yourself*   What kind of preparation helps us 'think it'? Which questions help us say our thoughts, releasing rather than inhibiting them?

2. *Saying for Others*   People may listen but this does not mean they hear. Telling our thoughts is a waste of time if the others don't hear what we're trying to say but only what they'd prefer us to say. What helps us listen?

3. *Saying Together*   Because we say and hear, does this mean we also 'know'? Does understanding also have to be articulated? In *Philosophy and the Young Child*, to which this writing owes a debt, Gareth B. Matthews quotes an anecdote about a child posing this dilemma:

Some question of fact arose between James and his father, and James said, 'I *know* it is!' His father replied, 'But perhaps you might

143

be wrong!' Dennis [four years, seven months] then joined in, saying, 'But if he knows, he can't be wrong! *Thinking*'s sometimes wrong, but *knowing*'s always right.' [p. 27]

Because a child utters a critically incisive comment, does that mean s/he *knows* what s/he means? What does the teacher do to consolidate *knowing* in both the sayer and the listeners? And how do we do this without spoiling the pleasure of the reading or the clarity of the saying?

4. *Saying the New*   What does the teacher say or do when the booktalk stimulates a 'new' thought? And how do we know a new thought when we hear one? For, we told ourselves constantly, we must remember that newness relates to children's understanding, not to our own. (Though, I must add, we adults frequently and gladly reported occasions when children gave us new thoughts. We learned an equality in booktalk which caused us to rethink our ideas about the relationship between teacher and taught.)

But Are Children Critics?

Baldly put to teacher colleagues, the answer is usually no. Criticism is regarded as an unnatural, specialist and adult activity for which you need training, as well as a perverse taste for pleasure-destroying analysis. Criticism, it seems, deals in abstractions, unfeeling intellectualism, cold-blooded dissection. You can't do criticism with children, and if you try you only put them off literature altogether. Many colleagues, it turned out, had been put off by what they thought of as criticism during secondary school and college literature courses.

We asked the question in the first place because our work persuaded us that children have an innate critical faculty. They instinctively question, report, compare, judge. Left to themselves they make plain their opinions and feelings, and are interested in the opinions and feelings of their friends. When they talk about books, films, television, sport, or whatever other own-time activities they share, they display all the enthusiastic discrimination of any adult connoisseur. No one, for example, is more detailed in his/her critical talk than a nine-year-old soccer fan comparing notes about the previous night's game, nor is more trenchant in defence of strongly held opinions.

If there is deep interest in a subject, and the facilities are provided for its expression, children are, it seems to us self-evident, natural critics from quite early ages (certainly by the time they come to school at five years old). What our adult colleagues were talking about, we decided, was a warped or damaged notion of the nature of literary criticism based upon their own unhappy experiences. What, then, did we think literary criticism is? What does a critic do? And is that what children do?

We began to listen more carefully to what children said, and to read more carefully what they wrote about books. We soon realized how much we do *not* notice, especially when working with large classes of thirty or more. Often children express themselves in rapid cut-and-thrust conversation that the teacher, concerned as much with keeping order and saying what s/he wants to say as with what the children are saying, misses the kernels of thought peppered through the conversation. We now try to record these moments of insight. First, because they are evidence of critical perception. Second, because they most clearly of all press upon us the question, 'What should the teacher do with the best things children say?'

Here are some examples that demonstrate what we mean, beginning with a saying I've used before but which still impresses me:

WILLIAM, aged ten, when asked if he didn't find Arthur Ransome's books rather long and 'slow' (I meant boring): 'Arthur Ransome is the sort of writer you enjoy most after you've finished him.'

This carries a number of possible meanings, all of them potent. William might be saying: When you are reading a richly made story, you experience the greatest pleasure only when you've finished reading, and can view the whole pattern of the book and see how everything fits together. Equally, he might be saying: All reading requires a certain expenditure of time and effort, energy and stamina. Books like Arthur Ransome's, because they are long, and detailed, take so much time and energy that for a while you wonder if it is worth going on. But if you persist and reach the end you feel all the greater enjoyment because of the satisfaction you get from 'seeing it through'. Like climbing a mountain, the kind of reading demanded by a long and densely written novel is hard work, but the view from the top makes it worth while and seems even better because of the hard work you've put in to get there.

If William meant something like this he was actually making a critically profound comment about reading itself, as well as about the nature of Ransome's stories. He might, of course, have been making a joke, on the lines of the one about banging your head against a brick wall—that Ransome's books are so tedious the only pleasure you get comes when you stop reading them. Which might be considered a critical comment of the same order as the others. As it is, we'll never know what he meant because I didn't ask him, and, typically of a child, he didn't feel it necessary to explain. Had I overcome my surprise at such a sophisticated idea so succinctly put, what, if anything, should I have 'done' with it?

HELEN, aged ten, when asked if she had found any 'boring bits' in my story, *The Present Takers*: 'I thought the first page and a half was boring and then I realized why it had to be.'

I have mentioned before (see page 130) the importance of locating the sites of boredom in the teaching of literature. Helen's remark invites her listeners' curiosity about what she means. But no one asked her, neither myself nor the nine or ten other children we were with. Can she have understood that her boredom precisely matches the passages in the book which establish the kind of story it is going to be, and how it should be read? Had she understood that literary boredom can be a matter of confusion, a period during reading when the reader is coming to grips with the demands of unfamiliar writing? If so, she had performed an astute act of criticism. Could she have excavated the site of her boredom and revealed its construction to herself and the rest of us? If so she would have demonstrated criticism at work. Would doing this have spoilt her pleasure and ours? Or would it, rather, have increased it? Was she, in fact, wanting us to ask her to show us what she meant? Did she only discover that she 'knew' what she meant when she said that sentence aloud, and at once wished she could try to make her meaning clear so that she could understand her own thought? No one can answer these questions with any certainty because no one, child or adult, knows. Our guess, after tentative explorations with children into their meaning when they say such things, is that they often do want to find out about, and understand, their critical insights.

MARK, a 'very limited ability' eight-year-old, after his class had been asked by their teacher if they could find any 'patterns' (the idea was explained) in *The Owl Who Was Afraid of the Dark* by Jill Tomlinson: 'There is a pattern in the way Plop goes along the branch each time, then falls off each time, and then meets another person each time.'

Mark is playing a game of 'I Spy'. He is discovering more or less hidden connections between various elements in the story, and finds enjoyment in doing so. A very great deal of critical activity, even of the most sophisticated kind, is about finding patterns—of language, of narrative 'codes', of plot events, of images, of character, and the rest. Where we focus our attention varies according to the nature of the story and the imperatives in our own reading of it. But all the time our experience shows that by finding patterns we make meaning, and that when we make meaning we experience pleasure. Mark may be of 'very limited ability' and only eight, but he is sharp-eyed as a reader and simply precise in saying what he has observed. The limitations of his (intellectual?) ability were no impediment to the exercise of his innate critical faculty given two facilitating aids. First, a choice of a book on which his faculty could operate. Second, a critically skilled and practised companion to whom he could apprentice himself as a critic, and who knew how and on what to help him focus his attention. Mark's companion was our colleague Barbara Raven, who translated an 'adult' act of structural analysis into a 'child enticing' game of 'I Spy'.

Nor is such discussion possible only with children already competent as readers or greatly practised at such talk, as this next example demonstrates.

SARAH, aged six, of *Railway Passage* by Charles Keeping: 'At the beginning some of the pictures are dull and at the end the pictures are coloured but one of the pictures isn't and that picture is one of Uncle Meanie and I think it is dark because it isn't happy.'

Sarah is learning to tell herself, and her friends, how stories work by looking at Keeping's subtly designed picture books, in which so many of the narrative codes are 'written' in the pictures. This way she is learning about literary complexity even before she can cope with linguistic complexity. And she is learning to do this with critical discrimination by saying out what she has noticed—'I Spy'—by hearing what others say, and by discussing their mutual observations.

I have not yet revealed what makes Sarah's saying even more striking. It was written. I have changed nothing except to provide capital letters for Uncle Meanie and an apostrophe for 'isn't'. Sarah would, however, have said it first to her teacher, then written it down for a 'real' purpose, not just as an exercise. This helped her sort out what she wanted to say and the order of her words before she tackled the task, difficult enough to demand all her concentration, of writing the words down. I was the 'real purpose' that provided the stimulus for such hard work; Sarah knew she was going to send her comments to an unknown adult, myself, who had a genuine interest in her thoughts about Keeping's books. Sarah is one of the makers of *A Book All About Books* described on page 25.

'The lion in *The Crane* is the same as the black rabbit in *Watership Down*,' our colleague Anna Collins reports one of her ten-year-old boys saying in a somewhat startling (and accurate?) example of children making connections and comparisons between their previous reading and their new, just as adult critics do. In her *Signal* article 'Them's for the Infants, Miss' Elaine Moss provides further evidence from eight- to eleven-year-olds talking about *Come Away from the Water, Shirley* by John Burningham and saying it is ' "Like *Peter Pan*, Miss", "No, like *Captain Pugwash*" '. She also relates how there were some children

> *at every age* who did not manage to make the jump across the 'gutter' from left-hand pages where the parents sit, occasionally addressing the unseen Shirley, to the right-hand pages on which Shirley is seen synthesizing a real rowing boat and stray dog on the shore into the fabric of her vivid daydream. . . . But far more children, again at all ages, did make the jump and were intrigued by the clues John Burningham laid for them. Although Shirley is not seen on the left-hand pages, 'She must have been there or her mum and dad wouldn't have kept talkin' to her, would they?'; 'Her body was there for them to tell not to do things, like "Don't play with that dog, you don't know where he's been", but her think was with the pirates.' [p. 68–69]

Shirley's body being there for her parents to order about but her think being with the pirates is a precise, if naïve, account of this story and the formal arrangement of the pictures across each doublespread that controls the narrative. And that this was understood by children of all ages, and by more of them than those who did not understand, further confirms our conviction that everyone is born with a critical faculty which we must then learn how to use with consciously ordered attention.

We could go on like this, building up anecdotal evidence in support of the view, increasingly strengthened by continuing experience, that all children are (or can be) critics. But saying this begs the questions, 'What is a critic?' and 'What does a critic do?' For answers, we took W. H. Auden's list given in his essay 'Reading' and quoted on page 20. This seemed to us an intelligent and useful summary. Now we asked, 'If children are indeed "natural" critics, how many of Auden's six functions can we show them fulfilling?' (We reminded ourselves that we meant children performing as critics for themselves, not necessarily for adults.)

1. There is no doubt that children introduce each other to unfamiliar authors. There are also times, each of us adults could testify, when children introduce authors to adults.

2. We had all experienced occasions when some children convinced others that they had undervalued a book. By chance on the very evening we discussed this point, Anna Collins had handed me some writing by her nine- and ten-year-olds after their discussion of *Sun Horse, Moon Horse* by Rosemary Sutcliff. 'I didn't really like the book or understand it until we had our talk. It made me understand a lot more,' one girl wrote, as if in answer to our question. 'I think,' wrote another, 'all the comments the people made made the story come alive for me, because I didn't get it at first'. And, as before, we adults found ourselves remembering times when our own opinions were revised by children's assessments.

3. This was harder to agree to at once. But we came to the conclusion that, among children, showing relations between works of different ages, etc., could and did happen. Certainly, however, it is usually an adult who shows children these relationships because the adult knows more about history and culture. But, we asked, was this simply because we didn't ever ask children to do this for themselves by helping them find the information? The question, 'What should the teacher do in booktalk?' raised itself again.

4. This relates to (2), and we had plenty of evidence to show that children give 'readings' which increase their own, and our adult, understanding of books. (An example of this happening occurs in the transcript on pages 160–8.)

5. We hesitated again; and again found ourselves asking why adults tend to 'throw light on the process of artistic "Making" ' for

children when we could see no reason why, sometimes at least, they should not explore this for themselves in the work of authors who particularly interest them. For my part, as an author who often visits classrooms, I can testify to the keen interest of children, certainly from the age of seven, when I show them how one of my books was 'made', using working papers from first, tentative idea to finished volume. Frequently, in return they tell me about their experience of writing, comparing it with mine, and are especially amused and fascinated by the similarities and differences, just as I am myself. I am often astonished at the clarity of some children's understanding of their own 'process of artistic "Making" '. That they can 'throw light' on the process to their own benefit I personally have no doubt. Apart from our own experience we find confirmation in published accounts like Donald H. Graves's *Writing: Teachers and Children at Work* and *The Tidy House* by Carolyn Steedman.

6. Here is six-year-old Paula throwing light on 'the relation of art to life' in her writing about Charles Keeping's *Charley, Charlotte and the Golden Canary* (this time in an unedited quotation):

> Charley and Charlotte were good friends and they played together by the bird stall I was sad when Charlotte went to the high block of flats and Charlottes mother no longer let Charlotte play I like playing with my friends and when I can't I feel upset. I feel sad because Jessica is going to leave our school and I will miss her very much.

And her classmate Katie on *Railway Passage*:

> Mrs Hopes read us a book about people who lived in the train cottages Here is my oppinion of it. there were two people were kind at the beginning of the book and they were still kind at the end. The money didnt make much difference to the people the miserable people got even more miserable after they had won the money. I think if I won a lot of money I would buy new clothes but I don't think I would be happy because I would wear them and they would get worn out and I would be miserable again

We could all recount occasions in booktalk when children moved from a discussion of the story itself to comment about related topics touched on by the story: money, family life, scientific information, moral and ethical problems, and so on. For example, when we studied children's responses to Philippa Pearce's *The Battle of Bubble and Squeak* we found that always there was a great deal of talk about the morality of Alice Sparrow's attempt to get rid of the gerbils by putting them out for the dustbin men to take away. This extended into a discussion of the rights of animals, and, by further extension (and bringing the talk back to the book), the rights of children as against parents and the rights of parents as against children. There was also talk about the natural history of gerbils (always one or two experts on this scientific subject) as well as numerous anecdotes about family arrangements and tensions, stimulated by relating Philippa Pearce's fictional family to their own real ones.

Indeed, we would criticize some teachers for using literature solely for this purpose, so easily do children engage in it. A novel like *My Mate Shofiq* by Jan Needle, for example, is all too often read with ten- and eleven-year-olds only because it controversially deals with racial prejudice and so causes heated talk about that subject. It is, in short, used like a social worker's case study or a documentary piece of journalism, as a starting point for investigation of a social issue. We disapprove of this because it leads to a misunderstanding about what literature is. Of course every work of literature involves a subject; but far more importantly it is a linguistic event, a metaphoric construct, a 'made' object, 'the illusion of a life in the mode of a virtual past' (Susanne Langer). ' "What takes place" in narrative,' Roland Barthes reminds us, 'is, from the referential (reality) point of view, literally *nothing*; "what happens" is language alone, the adventure of language, the unceasing celebration of its coming.' (Yes, he does mean to include the sexual connotation when he says 'its coming', as well as other possible interpretations.) It is this passionate adventure with language we want for our children. We therefore help them explore literature as its own story; and the story of literature is discovered in the story of our own and of others' reading of it. Literature is a linguistic construct, and our reading of it is a construct of the language we use in telling ourselves about our reading.

Judged by Auden's outline, then, children are indisputably critics. Our thinking-through of this led us to reconsider what literature is, and therefore what we, as teachers, should guide children to attend to in it. Because we acknowledge that literature is a Text held in language, and that the Text is experienced in an activity of production—production of the writing, production of the reading—we naturally seek to focus our children's attention above all (though not exclusively) on the production of their reading.

Our experience of helping children 'produce their reading' leads to some conclusions worth summarizing now:

1. Children of all ages are as various in their reading of a book as are adults. In any group some will concentrate on one feature, some on others. And though adults who have worked a lot with children can make intelligent guesses about the features that will be most attractive or rewarding, no one ever gets it completely right. On the contrary, any teaching that enables children in the uninhibited telling of their reading always gives the adult a surprise.

2. Underestimating the reading and critical capabilities of children is a difficult fault to change. Teachers especially have been trained to assume that 'stages of development' are common to all children of the same age, and to accept such notions as that children cannot distinguish between 'the real' and 'the fictional', the literal and the metaphoric, the ludic role of story and the irreversibly consequential finality of 'really doing it'. Such received opinions we challenge as not simply limiting but incorrect. We prefer instead to act on the assumption that children are potentially, if not actually, all that we are ourselves, and that in speaking out their own stories and their readings of other people's stories they 'talk themselves into being'. In telling their readings they activate their potentialities. But only if that reading is truly theirs and is shared, not just ours imposed upon them.

3. In any group of children, no matter what their supposed cleverness or lack of cleverness, we find that if they begin by sharing their most obvious observations we very soon accumulate a body of common wisdom that reveals to us the heart of a book and its meaning(s) for us all. Further, even when quite complicated or abstract ideas are approached this way (through story images and talked-out interpretations) there is little that children cannot grasp. In this activity as a whole there is a balance to be found between respect for the rights of the individual as a reader and talker, and the corporately composed reading of the group—the community Text, which is always more complex and insightful than any one individual reading.

This actively achieved balance in booktalk between the individual and the community is in itself, it seems to us, a lived metaphor of the truly egalitarian society. And, we would add, though we here discuss it in relation to children and its educational role, we find nothing different when we practise booktalk among ourselves or with other adults.

Which leads us now to put the question that brings us to the heart of our subject:

What do we say?

When we talk to others about our reading of a book we are telling something that happened to us—an experience of which we are so consciously aware that we can report it. Put another way, to tell the story of a reading is to describe a phenomenological event.

The phenomenology of reading has been well and briefly set out in Chapter Eleven of Wolfgang Iser's book *The Implied Reader*, and is given in great detail in his *The Act of Reading*. For our practical purposes we boiled down the teaching implications to one general principle: In talking with children about their reading we must mutually agree that *everything is honourably reportable*.

Why 'honourably' reportable? Because so often we have heard others as well as ourselves dismiss children's responses as 'wrong', 'irrelevant' or unhelpful. I describe an extreme example on page 130 in the story of 'The Boy Who was Bored'. By his reaction this teacher made it dishonourable to report any other response than that the book in question was enjoyable. He made everyone else feel that only his responses were honest, true and intelligent. Equally, much literature teaching proceeds as a game of 'Guess what's in teacher's head'. The children are asked a question about a book which may or may not have a single right answer, like the answer to an arithmetical sum, and the pupils suggest answers until somebody offers the one the teacher wants—the one already in his/her head. This reduces literary study to a kind of multiple-choice comprehension exercise with the teacher as a somewhat arbitrarily minded judge. (If we think few teachers now behave like this, we may congratulate ourselves on our own enlightenment but should also acknowledge that we seldom witness other teachers at work.)

More importantly, however, everything must be honourably reportable because in our revised practice the enjoyment and the study begins with the reader. We are seeking at least a glimpse of that 'first book', the Text the individual reader experienced; and out of these 'first books' contributed by the members of the class or group, we seek to create that larger book which belongs to us all. Both Texts are achieved in the same way. Wolfgang Iser describes the process in *The Implied Reader*:

> As we read, we oscillate to a greater or lesser degree between the building and the breaking of illusions. In a process of trial and error, we organize and reorganize the various data offered us by the text. These are the given factors, the fixed points on which we base our 'interpretation', trying to fit them together in the way we think the author meant them to be fitted. 'For to perceive, a beholder must *create* his own experience. And his creation must include relations comparable to those which the original producer underwent. They are not the same in any literal sense. But with the perceiver, as with the artist, there must be an ordering of the elements of the whole that is in form, although not in details, the same as the process of organization the creator of the work consciously experienced. Without an act of recreation the object is not perceived as a work of art.' (John Dewey, *Art as Experience*, New York, 1958, p. 54)
>
> The act of recreation is not a smooth or continuous process, but one which, in its essence, relies on *interruptions* of the flow to render it efficacious. We look forward, we look back, we decide, we change our decisions, we form expectations, we are shocked by their nonfulfilment, we question, we muse, we accept, we reject; this is the dynamic process of recreation. This process is steered by two main structural components within the text: first, a repertoire of familiar literary patterns and recurrent literary themes, together with allusions to familiar social and historical contexts; second, techniques or strategies used to set the familiar against the unfamiliar. [p. 288]

A child might put it another way. When Steve Bicknell asked a class of seven-year-olds how they felt after talking about a book (he meant talking in the way that we are here advocating), Wayne replied, 'You feel like you've had another story or the story over again.'

Booktalk, we think, should follow the 'dynamic process of recreation' Iser describes. In order for this to happen teachers must find a repertoire of questions that assist rather than hinder. Early on in our list-making we learned the benefit of banning from our speech, but not from the children's, the question *why?* Even when a child says something as simple as 'I liked this . . .' or 'I hated that . . .' the teacherly instinct is to ask why. The answer, more often than not, is a shaken head, shrugged shoulders, a loss of enthusiasm, a blank stare that hides a sudden sense of failure.

What's the trouble with *why*? Two things. First, telling what you like or dislike in a book is in itself an answer to the question why. You are explaining by example why you read as you did—with pleasure or boredom. Second, the question why so baldly asked is too big to answer. All the talk is itself an attempt, by answering more specific and manageable questions, finally to discover the answer to the ur-question *why*? Why life, why art, why this book instead of that, why do I feel as I do about this book, why do other people feel differently, and why this everlasting fascination with Story . . .?

By asking why the teacher confronts the child with the impossible. The magnitude of the task is so daunting the child gives up. The fun goes out of talking. We realize again how, so often in teaching, the best results are achieved by an oblique rather than a head-on approach. And that by posing manageable questions clearly in a game-playing—certainly in a play-full—manner, the answers to the unspoken ur-question are at least brought within range of speculation.

But how to avoid asking why? Our solution, when at last we hit upon it, was not only very simple, but proved a turning point in the reconsideration of our teaching methods, for it gave us a new style. We arrived at it by searching for what we thought of as 'a conversational glottal stop'. We meant an opening phrase that would prevent us asking why and would provide a broadly useful start to more specific questions.

The phrase we hit upon was: *Tell me* . . .

The quality we liked about 'Tell me . . .' was that it suggests collaboration, a desire by the teacher to know what a child thinks, and a conversational rather than an interrogational intent. Very soon 'Tell Me' became the mnemonic name we gave our still-developing method.

Now we set about compiling a list of 'Tell me . . .' questions which would be useful when we found ourselves during classroom booktalk wondering where to go next, or reverting in the press of the moment to our former ways. Our first compilation proved inadequate, this list being only of questions that aimed to help children talk about the phenomenology of their reading. But, we found, when a teacher is faced with a large group all wanting to share their readings, talk restricted to phenomenological questions can become unwieldy and amorphously anecdotal. It tends to stay on the two levels of retelling the narrative in their own words, and of matching themselves with the book-story by telling stories about their own lives.

An example. A class of ten-year-olds was talking about Emma Smith's *No Way of Telling* (an appropriate title under the circumstances). They were attracted by the idea of being snowbound, as the girl protagonist is. Soon they began telling equally exciting events in their own lives; and then went on to holiday anecdotes, from which they wandered into a discussion of what they would do if there was never any school and they could do as they liked all day. They found all this very entertaining. Afterwards their teacher was pleased because she felt they had talked well and that this in itself was valuable. Maybe so, but it wasn't booktalk. Emma Smith's novel and their reading of it had very little to do with what happened in class.

How to give coherence to the phenomenological reportage and at the same time maintain its literary function? The answer seemed to be that it must, from beginning to end, have a critical direction. We meant direction in both senses: the giving of order and clarity to what is said; and movement towards a known objective.

Deciding this presented us, of course, with a theoretical dilemma. We had argued ourselves into accepting that the teacher must 'get out of children's way' by not imposing a reading on them, but instead must facilitate their tellings of their own readings. Now we appeared to be saying that the teacher must shape the children's reportage by giving it a critical direction which, presumably, the teacher will have decided on before the talk starts.

Trying out the 'Tell Me' approach on ourselves soon demonstrated that the dilemma did not actually exist. One evening we took 'The Star', a story from Alasdair Gray's book *Unlikely Stories, Mostly*. We each read it silently, heard it read aloud by one of us, and then spent a few minutes jotting down notes of anything that had impressed us or seemed interesting and which we wanted to remember for our talk. (This was by now our standard practice as preparation for book discussions.) Acting as 'teacher', I had prepared myself before the meeting, and had decided on the 'critical direction' I thought should guide the talk. And so we began, following the 'Tell Me' list of questions as then compiled. As we went along we monitored our conversation, watching for the critical cues our phenomenological reportage offered, and noting how these fitted into, or required adaptation of, my prepared preferences.

'The Star' is very short: three modest pages, including two half-page black-and-white line illustrations that are not just decorative but are integral to the words. They add information and are carefully 'laid into' the words themselves. The style is plain. Here is the opening:

A star had fallen beyond the horizon, in Canada perhaps. (He had an aunt in Canada.) The second was nearer, just beyond the iron works, so he was not surprised when the third fell into the backyard. [p. 1]

The protagonist, we can see from the illustration, is a short-trousered boy of about ten. He goes in search of the third star, finds it, takes it to bed, looks at it under the bedclothes, finding 'the grandest thing he had ever seen . . . an ocean of glittering blue-black waves under a sky full of huge galaxies', as well as other astonishments. Next day he takes the star to school, is caught with it by a harsh teacher, and when asked to give it up, swallows it. 'Teacher, classroom, world receded like a rocket into a warm, easy blackness leaving behind a trail of glorious stars, and he was one of them.'

Our talk at once fixed on the pictures; but soon we found linking ideas between the pictures and the words. These led us to notice patterns: of sound (labials); of coming from a distance to a close-up so near it ends inside (a star from space comes finally into the boy's body) and outwards again (from inside of house to school to space); patterns of colour and shape (the patterns the boy sees in the star); and so on. These observations pointed us to hints of meaning, negotiating agreement about which kept us busy for a long time. Some of these notions I had included in my preparation; but some came new to me. The interesting thing was that questions about how the story was told kept us returning to the text, kept us concentrated on the story and the way the meaning was being made.

Of course, we supposed that our talk had gone like this because of our familiarity with critical conversation. We were not at all persuaded that children would deal with the story in quite the same way. In fact, to our surprise, our classes followed just the same critical path, even though we restrained ourselves from any attempt to guide their talk, but simply posed questions which asked them to tell us what they had noticed in the story. They too began with the pictures; they too found connections between the pictures and the words; they too, most excitingly of all, began finding patterns. And from their pattern-finding they went on to seek out meaning, and to argue about their individual resolutions of meaning, just as we adults had done.

It was at this point, in the resolution of meaning, that the adult was needed in the teacherly role of guiding attention. For some children tried to resolve the story into meanings that were against the information plainly given in the narrative. Before this, the teacher's role was that of chairperson, who posed the questions that take the place of an agenda, and ensured that anyone who wanted to speak would not be swamped by the more dominant members of the class. From time to time we would need to clarify a point because a child had said it awkwardly. At these times we would use a conversational device which suggests but doesn't threaten: 'Do you mean . . .?' Thus: 'When you say you don't like the schoolteacher, do you mean he is not a likeable person, or do you mean you don't think he's very well described?'

What we found was that the dilemma was not a problem, not a question of an either/or choice at all, but was simply a matter of balance. The teacher is both facilitator *and* guide. There is, for sure, no escaping the burden of the fact that the teacher must teach. In literary education, for example, the teacher finally decides which literature shall be read and shared. Undoubtedly the desires of the taught will be taken into account; but in the end the teacher chooses because it is a teacherly responsibility to do so. And that decision is made on the basis of prior decisions about the literary qualities possessed by the book the teacher wants the taught to engage with. This is, in other words, a critically based judgement which also cannot be escaped. But equally, as the readers report their readings, the teacher must be attentive to the critical suggestions proposed (not always consciously) by the readers and be prepared to adapt his/her prepared understandings in the light of the readers' insights. This too is a teacherly responsibility requiring, we readily acknowledge, training, skill, and experience.

Indeed, the whole account of our argument is that if children are enabled in the 'production of their reading', their talk will itself focus on critically important features of the book, which it is then the teacher's role to highlight so that the children come to a conscious understanding of their discoveries and the nature of the experience the writing makes available to them. Furthermore, we are arguing, in this kind of talk any group of readers—whether children or adults—make enough critically perceptive comments to carry the talk to the heart of the text and its possible meanings.

A Sample

We want to show this happening. But there is not space for a full-scale transcript of a complete booktalk session. However, we can, in at least a brief extract, give a sample of our 'Tell me' approach in action. What follows are segments from an hour-long session recorded in Jan Maxwell's classroom. The segments show the beginning of the talk, during which children reported without comment or explanation their early impressions; then follow passages from the moment when this straightforward reportage shifted into a phase of puzzle-sharing and speculation about meaning; and finally comes a longer section from the middle of the session, when the children began finding patterns and connections, which took them to the core of the book.

There were twenty-three eight-year-old children in the group. The book they talked about was *The Crane* by Reiner Zimnik. This was the first occasion that Jan tried out the first version of the Framework, though her children were used to talking with her about their reading. The session took place towards the end of a summer term. Jan set the scene in a note written for our study group:

I read from the hardback edition, showing the children the whole book before we started and all the graphics as we proceeded. I read the whole story before we had any discussion, which was not our normal pattern, and the children, I felt, found this rather strange; there were occasions when I specifically had to stop them commenting and questioning. I had hoped to read the story within a complete week, a passage each day, but unfortunately we were interrupted and the reading wasn't finished until the second week.

We held our discussion the day after I finished reading and we sat, uncharacteristically, on chairs, in a circle by the blackboard. This is something I would *not* do again—it made the whole thing too formal and opened up a rather forbidding space between us. For my own reference I tape-recorded the discussion, but wish in retrospect that I had made notes as well—I relied too much on the recording to act as my memory.

I followed the Framework by using the questions:

1. What did you first notice about the book?
2. Which parts did you like?
3. Which parts puzzled you?
4. Did you notice any patterns/links?

These questions followed on naturally from one another so that I omitted the questions about boring parts and parts the children did not like.

The second question produced certain concrete incidents as most popular but then led on to the question of the silver lion and the crane driver's dream (not linked together). These two incidents/characters had also aroused the greatest degree of puzzlement. The crane driver's dream in particular dominated the conversation for a long time and led the children to consider the nature of the relationships between the crane driver and Lektro, and the crane driver and the eagle. Some of the children became bogged down with the idea that Lektro had changed into the eagle, others thought that Lektro's spirit had entered into the eagle. The dream was obviously a very significant event, and led quite naturally into a search for links and patterns. Here the children linked the silver lion with something good and the ravens, sharks and rider of death with something evil.

We talked for nearly an hour and could have gone on if lunchtime had not intervened! A total of fifteen children out of twenty-three made contributions, all of them thoughtful and relevant. Had we been sitting in our normal informal group I think more children would have talked.

In transcribing Jan's tape I have not noted hesitations and false starts; and sometimes the tape is indecipherable where outside noise broke through. Throughout, however, one of the things that impressed me was the clarity and assurance of the children's speech, a tribute to Jan's teaching. Perhaps it is also worth mentioning that no child was required to speak; Jan picked out the next speaker from those indicating they were ready.

JAN   I want you to . . . See if you can remember, and tell me what you thought when you first saw the book . . . Clare.
CLARE   It looked quite good but it seems a sort of boys' book, and the pictures on the front . . . it looked interesting and when we

got a little way into it I began to think, 'Oh, this is a children's story.'

JAN   Timothy.

TIMOTHY   Well, I thought it was all about a crane and how they build it and what they used to build it and things, and so I thought it would be quite boring.

JAN   Daniel.

DANIEL   At the beginning it seemed like they were going to take a really long time to build the crane and then they were going to make the adventures . . . [Indecipherable.]

NICHOLAS   I thought it was just going to be on building the crane.

[Tracey speaks. Indecipherable.]

RICHARD   Well, when I first saw it I thought it was going to be all about the building of the crane and all about the loading of the crane. The crane loading things into ships and how the actual place built up into a famous place.

JAN   Helen.

HELEN   I thought it was going to be quite boring.

[It is generally agreed that these expectations were the ones shared by everyone.]

JAN   Tell me about which bits you liked. Timothy.

TIMOTHY   It was when he was lifting the town councillors across the river and he was shaking them about. And they all had bacon and egg for lunch.

JAN   Emma.

EMMA   I liked it when they had finished the flood and the animals started to come again.

JAN   Did you? Yes. Clare.

CLARE   I'll tell you what I thought it was like at the beginning. It was quite nice, then it . . . I think the bit where I began to really get interested in it was where the crane driver actually put the splints made of fish bone in the eagle's broken wing. Then when they found out the man in the potato field and when he actually came down with a sack of potatoes. I thought that was the best bit.

JAN   Mm! Peter.

PETER   I think it was quite good when the elephant had sunstroke. He was running about . . . [laughter] . . . and the crane picked him up and dipped him in and out of the water to calm him down.

JAN   Yes. What a lot of different bits there are, aren't there! . . . Daniel.

So the talk proceeds, increasing in pace and enthusiasm as other speakers mention the eagle, Lektro, Lektro and the silver lion, and the little fishes swimming through holes in the shark. The important point for me is that in telling about their expectations and about the things they liked the children have already offered cues for consideration of the main features of the book: its comic, surreal quality; and the formal relationships between such elements as dream and 'reality', the characters in the story and symbolically dramatic presences like the silver lion. Jan doesn't pick these up straightaway, however. She leaves them alone, till the children rediscover them later. This rediscovery begins when Timothy fastens on Nathan's mention of the little fishes swimming through the shark.

TIMOTHY   I like it the same as Nathan because it seems a bit strange and I think that's the bit that I think makes me like the story.

Immediately the idea of strangeness is taken up. Jan allows this reportage to continue for five or six minutes before she asks if there were things they didn't like. Clare says that she didn't like the crane driver's salary, as it wasn't fair! Timothy didn't like it when Lektro kept appearing and disappearing while talking to the crane driver (another of the dream elements). This leads to a discussion that Jan finally sums up, clearly feeling the time has come to direct attention to problems of form.

JAN   Timothy said it was unfair when Lektro kept appearing and then going away again. Clare said she thinks that that was a dream, and Tracey said that she thinks it did mention something about a dream. Timothy said it couldn't have been a dream because he didn't go to sleep. What do the rest of you think?

There follows a period of hesitation. It is as if no one quite knows what to say next. An anxious or inexperienced teacher might, at this point, change tack, returning to more secure subjects. But Jan waits, allowing everyone time for thought, while a few comments are made of no apparent importance. Her patience is rewarded by a boy who suddenly interrupts the subdued flow:

BOY   I just realized that since Lektro died he could have been a spirit.
JAN   Mm . . . yes . . . Had you forgotten that he'd died?
BOY   Yes.

This remembering causes Clare, in a passage too damaged by extraneous noise for accurate transcription, to suggest that the eagle and the silver lion might also be spirits. She suggests that because the eagle appears at the time Lektro is appearing and disappearing, the eagle might be Lektro's spirit.

They discuss this, eventually returning to the text in order to establish the precise order and relationship of events. Jan reads the key passage out. They discuss it, puzzling out a resolution to the problem of the eagle's true identity. This becomes so difficult that they begin again to talk about parts they didn't like: in other words, they concentrate on difficulty, and do so by constant reference to what the text actually says. All sorts of suggestions are made. Jan squashes none of them.

A head of steam builds up that must inevitably lead to a desire for some meaningful connection to be found between these so far unconnected elements. Jan waits for this moment to arrive, which eventually it does in this way:

RICHARD   I didn't like the part where the ravens were laughing. The ravens were always cruel and they were always jealous of the crane driver.
JAN   They were, weren't they? Yes. Roger.
ROGER   This may sound silly but when they were laughing at the crane driver they might have changed into the sharks to try and knock down the crane.
JAN   That's just reminded me of another question I was going to ask you, and I think that all this fits together somehow. I was going to ask you this question. Remember when we were doing our work about patterns, and I read you fairy stories, and we were looking for patterns in the stories? Now I was going to ask you if you can see patterns . . . or connections . . . in this book? Can you think of things that kind of make a pattern? Now, I think from what Roger

has said, I have just begun to see the beginning of a pattern. I think. I'm not sure, because I'm trying to work this out the same as you are. And I think I can begin to see a pattern that says . . . [writing on board] . . . RAVENS . . . [indecipherable] . . .

CHILDREN   Sharks!

JAN   [writing] SHARKS. Ravens and sharks. Can you see what I'm beginning to see? Clare?

CLARE   Well, I don't think of the two things—the ravens were laughing and then the sea floods the land, then the sharks strike, then they went back and changed again, so I think the next thing which can be [seen in?] my mind is sharks and when the sea's been drained away they were able to [indecipherable] again. So I think it goes: ravens, sharks, sharks, ravens.

JAN   Ravens, sharks, sharks, ravens. Yes. Can you think of anything that would add to that pattern? Anything else in the book that goes with ravens and sharks?

[Indecipherable.]

JAN   Yes, try and think more carefully about why they would fit the pattern about ravens and sharks. Or whether they *would* fit the pattern! Tracey.

TRACEY   It might not fit the pattern, but the ravens [indecipherable] first, then there came the wars and then the floods and then the sharks begin to come in. That was probably what they were laughing about.

JAN   So we can see RAVENS, WAR, FLOOD, SHARKS. Roger?

ROGER   After the ravens have stopped laughing and the war was about to start, before it started the crane driver could see Death riding on the horses.

JAN   Um, that's right! Remember that piece?

CHILDREN   Yes!

JAN   He saw Death riding on a horse, didn't he! Timothy?

TIMOTHY   I disagree with Roger because I think it said when the sharks were around the ravens were still looking with him. So they couldn't have turned into sharks.

[Numerous comments amongst each other as they try to establish the truth of this.]

JAN   Roger, did you actually say that the ravens changed into sharks?

ROGER   Well . . . yes!

164

JAN Do you still think so? [Tentatively]: Or are you beginning to change your mind . . . or . . .?

ROGER Well . . . yes . . . I am.

JAN What do the rest of you think about that? Timothy said he disagreed because . . .?

TIMOTHY I think it said that the ravens were there when they could see the sharks.

JAN Clare, what do you think, please?

CLARE Well, I disagree with both of them entirely. One thing, they . . . Roger may be right . . . but . . . Two things. You said that they were around and as Chris said, they might have got suffocated by the spirit, but if they had been survivors how would they have been able to build nests and have young? 'Cos ravens don't live that long and they . . . [indecipherable] . . . how they picked up nesting materials?

[Pause]

JAN [searching through the book] I'm trying to find . . .

RICHARD I disagree, Clare, because, remember they had that potato field around. Now they *might* have . . . you know, the eagle had stored up [indecipherable] to fly to see what was over, so the ravens may have been able to fly over there and get nesting . . .

CLARE No, I don't think so, Richard. They aren't [indecipherable]. But anyway the eagle could get near the mountains . . . he got near the mountains but he couldn't get *over* the mountains.

JAN No, he couldn't!

CLARE He just saw the sharks. And as that was as far as the eagle could fly, and an eagle can fly very very far, I do *not* think ravens would be able to [indecipherable]. I really don't!

JAN Let's just think—going back to patterns, Clare. The ravens come in more than once, don't they?

CHILDREN Yes!

JAN The sharks come in more than once.

CHILDREN Yes!

JAN Can you think of anything else that makes a pattern in that sort of way? We've got ravens, we've got the sharks. Can you think of any other things?

[Pause]

JAN Tracey.

TRACEY I think, about the ravens, I think I kind of disagree with Clare and then I don't disagree. I don't disagree with Clare a lot, but I don't see how the ravens can have changed into the sharks because, Clare, if they had got suffocated, some of them, there were more than a hundred sharks around, how could all the ravens change into all those many sharks?

JAN So you don't think the ravens changed into the sharks?

TRACEY No.

JAN I think that's what most of us would say.

CHILDREN Yes!

JAN Is there a connection between ravens and sharks? Ann.

ANN Um . . . no.

PETER Were the sharks black, 'cos ravens are black?

CHILDREN No!

A BOY They're obviously killer sharks, 'cos they couldn't be attacking where people were.

JAN Yes . . . so . . .? Clare.

CLARE Well, there is a connection. It's got nothing to do with colour or anything. They're both in a way *evil*. The ravens had wicked looks in their eyes and were cackling all the time. And the sharks were very wicked looking and they were trying to kill people. There is a point there. [Indecipherable.]

JAN There's a connection in that they're both evil, isn't there? Timothy.

TIMOTHY I disagree with Clare when she said they couldn't build nests very well because there would be not much sticks, but I disagree with that because bombs and things might have scattered sticks and things quite a lot.

JAN All over the place! Yes, that's quite true! [Indecipherable.]

RICHARD I think that ravens possibly could have changed into sharks because it seems as though Lektro changed into the eagle.

JAN Well, we must think about that as well. We must decide whether we think Lektro *really* changed into the eagle. Nicholas.

NICHOLAS I was thinking about the ravens. I was thinking if the river pirates escaped from gaol they might have changed into them.

JAN You think the river pirates might have changed into the ravens?

NICHOLAS Yes.

[Daniel now causes a disagreement about Lektro and the eagle which is resolved by reference to the text.]

JAN Is there a connection *in some way* between the eagle and

Lektro? Clare said there's a connection between the ravens and the sharks because they're evil. Is there a connection between Lektro and the eagle?

[Clare tries again to establish that the one turned into the other.]

JAN Think about this very carefully, about whether they are really changing into something else, or whether there's just a connection between them, like there's a connection between the ravens and the sharks. Do you have to say that the ravens changed into the sharks?

CHILDREN No!

JAN Can we not just say there is a connection between the ravens and the sharks because they're both evil?

CHILDREN Yes.

JAN Does it make sense of the story?

CHILDREN Yes!

JAN Now, what about Lektro and the eagle? Is there a connection? Timothy.

TIMOTHY I think they could both be good. 'Cos they could both be on the ship.

JAN Let's put this down. [Writing on board]: LEKTRO and the EAGLE. Good. What have they got to do with the crane driver? Clare.

CLARE Two things. Lektro was a good friend of the crane driver, and the eagle was. They both had good [indecipherable.]

JAN Now we've got LEKTRO and the EAGLE and the RAVENS and SHARKS. Can you see any other patterns that come up? Tracey.

[Indecipherable.]

JAN Does the silver lion make a kind of pattern?

CHILDREN A bit!

JAN A bit! Yes. How? Clare.

CLARE Well, the river pirates are bad and the silver lion is good.

JAN [at the board] So the silver lion fits into this bit, with Lektro and the eagle, all the good things, doesn't he? So he was good. And we've got the . . . on the bad, we've got the ravens, the sharks, and death—the figure of death—

[Overtalking.]

JAN Now we've got three things on each side. The ravens, the sharks and the figure of death. And here we've got Lektro and eagle and silver lion. Now, can we see a connection between any

167

of those. I'm beginning to see things, I think. [Pause.] Richard.
RICHARD   Well, obviously, you could say the ravens and Lektro
go together, silver lion can be maybe a spirit, and death must be a
sort of spirit, so silver lion and death can go together.
JAN   That's quite interesting, 'cos that's what I was thinking.
Certainly, silver lion and death are kinds of spirit. Where the other
things are real things, silver lion and the figure of death are not
real, are they, somehow?
CHILDREN   No!
JAN   So they have a different sort of meaning from the others,
don't they? Because death comes along when war is coming and
. . . silver lion comes in more than once, doesn't he?
CHILDREN   Yes.
CLARE   So does the figure of death, because he comes before the
war but comes after.
JAN   That's right, Clare, he does. He does indeed! Silver lion
comes when? Daniel.
[Indecipherable.]
JAN   Yes. Let's try and think of the times when silver lion comes.
He comes before the war, on the landing. Can you remember
exactly when?
A BOY   Was it after the crane driver had been helping the circus
people with the animals?
JAN   Yes, it was.
CHILDREN   Yes!
[They sort this out precisely, listing the lion's appearances.]

A narrative pattern is being discovered and reconstructed. The class
is within range of a recuperation of meaning, and in the final part of
the lesson they began sorting this out. Quite obviously, from the time
Jan first mentioned the ravens we can see from the transcript the
critical direction she had in mind. But all the time she works through
the features noted by the children and mentioned when they reported
their reactions. And, as she told us, in doing this she found herself
gaining new insights because of what her children said.

'Tell Me': The Framework

If there should be a critical direction in booktalk, which direction
should we take (there are, after all, many possible directions to
choose from), and which questions should be asked? It was in our

shared reading of Roland Barthes (particularly *The Pleasure of the Text* and *S/Z*) and in my reported reading of Gérard Genette's *Narrative Discourse* (the study of narrative modes being, as I write, one of the growing points of our discussions) that we found the critical direction which best accorded with the direction our own booktalk seemed most usually to take. At the same time, our study of novels like Italo Calvino's *If on a Winter's Night a Traveller* and Graham Swift's *Waterland*, alongside children's stories—Philippa Pearce's *The Battle of Bubble and Squeak*, Alan Garner's *The Stone Book*, Anthony Browne's picture books, Maurice Sendak's *Outside Over There*—and the poetry of Ted Hughes and Charles Causley, provided contexts for our practical exploration of critical theory.

Out of this mix we shaped our questions, which bring into play two controlling elements:

Some questions are *phenomenological* in nature. They lead the reader to report 'what happened'—thoughts, feelings, observations—during and since his/her reading.

Some questions are *structural* in nature (though not narrowly structuralist). They focus on 'How the story is told', on form, and not on 'What the story is about', on content. It is our contention that leading the reader to discuss formal questions leads naturally to a consideration of content. Coming at content through form keeps us in touch with 'the work'—the book that can be held in the hand. And through 'the work' we concentrate on the Text—that ever-changing *gestalt* which is held in language, and which is the creative heart of literature. Concentration on content alone leads, on the one hand, to the kind of non-literary talk we described earlier, while, on the other hand, it leads to the posing of what are little more than comprehension questions about character, plot, theme and meaning of the kind which have often deadened literature teaching in secondary schools.

Our questions, in short, focus on the reader's experience of the text, and lead the reader to understand and appreciate that experience by considering the way the Text was formed by the writing.

In doing this we found, to our excitement, and at first to our surprise, that children of all school ages not only enjoyed themselves but became, session by session, ever more articulate, ever more perceptive, ever more discriminatingly critical in their talk.

Here are the questions that presently make up the Framework. Of course, each of them is adapted and rephrased to suit the children we work with.

Tell me . . . When you first saw the book, even before you read it, what kind of book did you think it was going to be?
> Can you tell me what made you think this?
> Now you've read it, is it like what you expected?

Tell me about anything that particularly caught your attention.

What will you tell your friends about it?
> What won't you tell them, because it might spoil the story for them or be misleading if you did?

Tell me about the parts you liked most.

Tell me about the parts you didn't like.
> Were there parts that bored you?
> If you gave up reading, can you tell me where you stopped?
> I wonder what stopped you?

Was there anything that puzzled you?
> Was there anything you thought strange?
> Was there anything that took you by surprise?

Have you ever read other books/stories/poems like this?
> Tell me about them.
> What sticks in your memory most vividly?
> Can you tell me how they are alike? And how they are different?

Was this a story you read quickly? All in one go? Or slowly? And in separate sessions?
> Would you like to read it again? [If yes]: Would you read it differently next time?
> When you're reading, do you hear the words being said in your head? If so, whose voice is it you hear?

Which character interested you the most?
> Is that character the most important person in the story?

Or is it really about someone else?

Which character(s) didn't you like?

Did any of the characters remind you of people you know?

Who was telling the story? Do we know?

I wonder if it would make any difference if we did know/ didn't know that someone else in the story told it?

Did you notice things in the story/the poem that made a pattern? [If pattern-making is a strange idea then preparatory work should be done before the reading. And an example given by the teacher helps, as Jan Maxwell does in the transcript passage on page 163.]

[Alternatively]: Let's play a game of 'I Spy'. I'll start. I spy [give example]. Now your turn. [The game is played until sufficient elements that form one narrative pattern are discovered, and the readers are then invited to suggest the pattern and to set about finding more.]

How long did it take for the story to happen?

Did we find out about the story in the order the events happened?

When you tell about things that happen to you, do you always tell your story in the right order? Are there sometimes reasons why you don't? Can you tell me what they are?

Are there parts of the story that took a long time to happen but which are told about very quickly? And are there parts that happened very quickly but took a lot of space to tell about?

When you were reading the story did you feel it was happening now? Or did you feel it was happening in the past and being remembered?

Can you tell me about anything in the writing that made you feel like that?

Did you feel as if everything were happening to you, as if you were one of the characters in the story? Or did you feel as if you were an observer, watching what was happening but not part of the action?

If you were an observer, where were you watching from? Did you seem to watch from different places—sometimes, perhaps, from beside the characters, sometimes from above them as if you were in a helicopter? Can you tell me places in the book where you felt like that?

Has anything like this ever happened to you? Did you feel the same as the people in the story?

Where did the story happen?
Did it matter where it happened or could it have happened anywhere? Do you remember thinking about the place as you were reading?

Did we ever get to know what the characters were thinking about?
One of the characters [name] thought thus-and-such. Do you agree with him/her?

When you're reading a story do you see it happening in your imagination?
What kinds of details in the story help you see it most clearly? Tell me some of them.

If the author asked you what could be improved in the story, what would you say?

We've listened to each others' thoughts about the story, and heard all sorts of things about what we've each noticed. Are you surprised by anything someone else said?
Has anyone said anything that has changed your mind? Or helped you enjoy the story more? Or helped you understand it better?
Tell me about the things people said that struck you the most.

Has anyone read this story before? [If so]: Tell me, was it different this time?
Did you notice anything this time you didn't notice the first time?
Did you enjoy it more or less?
Because of what happened to you the second time, would you recommend other people to read it again as well, or isn't the story worth it?

When you think of this story now, after all we've said, what is the most important thing about it for you?

Do you think I should give this book to other people? Should I give it to people your age or older, or younger?

> How should I give it to them? Should I read it aloud, or tell them about it, or let them read it for themselves? What would be best for the story and for the readers?
> Should we talk about it afterwards, as we have done, or not?
> Do you know people who you think would especially like it?

This may seem a long list. So perhaps we should point out the obvious. We don't intend that every question be used every time. Nor do we expect to plod through the questions in the order set out here. The first couple of questions get us started, and then we are led by the answers the children give.

In fact, our experience is that after a while the Framework sinks into the backs of our minds; we don't consciously use it at all. 'It makes the whole book discussion much more open-ended,' Jan Maxwell noted, 'and gives far greater scope for the development and expression of the children's own ideas and feelings.' And Anna Collins added, 'It gives a greater feeling of confidence. But I haven't used it verbatim. Rather, it shapes my thoughts and points me to what I'm listening for.' Steve Bicknell wrote that 'Each time we talked about a book I found I needed to refer to the Framework less and less frequently. I didn't need notes by my side. I also became aware that certain questions did not need to be put—the children started the discussions themselves, usually talking about likes, dislikes and boredom.'

One more important point. Nowhere do we ask about meaning. Asking about meaning is like asking 'Why?' It is a dead end. Understanding about meaning is arrived at naturally as the more specific and practical questions about 'what happened to us as we read?' and 'how is the story told?' are discussed. Thus we can say that content and meaning are best approached through exploration of form and pattern.

So much here to discuss! We realize the next phase of our work must be the detailed consideration of a number of complete transcripts so that we can explore what happened in our lessons, and what we can learn from them about children as critics, about ourselves as teachers, and about literature as a mode of discourse. We shall keep an interested eye on other people's inquiries. And of course we shall go on enjoying our own private reading together, not just because this is a great pleasure, but because we think that what we are as readers ourselves is the foundation of our work as teachers of other readers.

We know that we are engaged in something, the implications of which are far from fully understood, either by ourselves or by other teachers. And because we regard Story and literary reading as the creative heart of all education, we propose the importance of seeking for that understanding.

An extract from Steve Bicknell's end-of-year letter about his use of the Framework began this record of six teachers teaching each other. We would like to use another extract to end it, because what Steve says sums up what we all felt after our first uses of this approach.

> Eight-year-old Sarah: 'We don't know what we think about a book until we've talked about it.'
>
> I doubt very much whether Sarah would have managed such a profound statement earlier in the school year and, to be perfectly honest, I'm not convinced that she would have been *able* to say it had she been in earlier classes of mine. I think it would be realistic to claim that the style of conversation that evolved in my classroom after I'd started using the Framework enabled children to see books in a different and more complete way.

*

POSTSCRIPT   This from Roland Barthes' *The Pleasure of the Text* [pp. 14 and 15] as final word to article and *Booktalk*:

> *Society of the Friends of the Text*: its members would have nothing in common (for there is no necessary agreement on the texts of pleasure) but their enemies: fools of all kinds, who decree foreclosure of the text and of its pleasure, either by cultural conformism or by intransigent rationalism (suspecting a 'mystique' of literature) or by political moralism or by criticism of the signifier or by stupid pragmatism or by snide vacuity or by destruction of the discourse, loss of verbal desire. Such a society would have no site, could function only in total atopia; yet it would be a kind of phalanstery, for in it contradictions would be acknowledged (and the risks of ideological imposture thereby restricted), difference would be observed, and conflict rendered insignificant (being unproductive of pleasure).

Notes and References

Books and articles quoted from
or otherwise referred to

W. H. Auden, 'Reading' in *The Dyer's Hand and Other Essays*, Faber & Faber, 1963

Roland Barthes, *Image-Music-Text* (ed. Stephen Heath), Fontana/ Collins, 1977

Roland Barthes, *The Pleasure of the Text*, Hill & Wang, New York, 1975

Roland Barthes, *S/Z*, Hill & Wang, New York, 1974

Wayne C. Booth, *The Rhetoric of Fiction*, University of Chicago Press, 1961

Lucy Boston, in *A Sense of Story* by John Rowe Townsend, Longman, 1971

Lucy Boston, *The Children of Green Knowe*, Faber & Faber, 1954; quoted from the Faber paperback, 1963

Lucy Boston, *Yew Hall*, Bodley Head, 1972. First published Faber & Faber, 1954

Kenneth Burke, *The Philosophy of Literary Form*, Vintage, New York, 1967

Dorothy Butler, *Cushla and Her Books*, Hodder & Stoughton, 1979

Lewis Carroll, *Through the Looking-Glass*, Macmillan, 1872; quoted from New Children's Edition, Macmillan, 1980

Aidan Chambers, *Fox Tricks*, Heinemann, 1980

Aidan Chambers, *Introducing Books to Children*, second edition, Horn Book, Boston, 1983. First published Heinemann Educational Books, 1973

Aidan Chambers, *The Reluctant Reader*, Pergamon, 1969

Jonathan Culler, *On Deconstruction: Theory and Criticism After Structuralism*, Routledge & Kegan Paul, 1983

Roald Dahl, 'The Champion of The World' in *Kiss Kiss*, Michael Joseph 1960; quoted from the Penguin paperback, 1962

Roald Dahl, *Danny: The Champion of the World*, Jonathan Cape, 1975

David Daiches, *Critical Approaches to Literature*, Prentice-Hall, New Jersey, 1956

John Fowles, *Daniel Martin*, Jonathan Cape, 1977

Hans-Georg Gadamer, *Truth and Method*, Sheed & Ward, 1975

Alan Garner, in *The Reluctant Reader* by Aidan Chambers, Pergamon, 1969

Gérard Genette, *Narrative Discourse*, Basil Blackwell, 1980

Donald Graves, *Writing: Teachers and Children at Work*, Heinemann Educational Books, 1983

Alasdair Gray, 'The Star' in *Unlikely Stories, Mostly*, Canongate, 1983

Richard Hoggart, 'Finding a Voice' in *Speaking to Each Other*, Vol. 2, *About Literature*, Chatto & Windus, 1970

Wolfgang Iser, *The Act of Reading: A Theory of Aesthetic Response*, Routledge & Kegan Paul, 1978

Wolfgang Iser, *The Implied Reader: Patterns of Prose Fiction from Bunyan to Beckett*, Johns Hopkins, Baltimore, 1974

Franz Kafka, *Briefe 1902–1924*, Frankfurt, 1958; quoted from *The Modern English Novel: The Reader, the Writer and the Work* (ed. Gabriel Josipovici), Open Books, 1976

Frank Kermode, *Essays on Fiction 1971–82*, Routledge & Kegan Paul, 1983

Alvin Kernan, in *The 'Revels' History of Drama in English*, Vol. III, 1576–1613, by J. Leeds Barroll, Alexander Leggatt, Richard Hosley, and Alvin Kernan, Methuen, 1975

F. H. Langman, 'The Idea of the Reader in Literary Criticism' in *The British Journal of Aesthetics*, January 1967

Gareth B. Matthews, *Philosophy and the Young Child*, Harvard University Press, Boston, 1980

William Mayne, *A Game of Dark*, Hamish Hamilton, 1971

James Moffett, *Teaching the Universe of Discourse*, Houghton Mifflin, Boston, 1968

Elaine Moss, 'Them's for the Infants, Miss', Part 1, *Signal* 26, May 1978

Arthur Ransome, in *Chosen for Children*, Library Association, 1967

Arthur Ransome, *Swallows and Amazons*, Jonathan Cape, 1930; quoted from Puffin paperback, 1962

Charles Sarland, 'Chorister Quartet', *Signal* 18, September 1975

Carolyn Steedman, *The Tidy House: Little Girls Writing*, Virago, 1982

Laurence Sterne, *The Life and Opinions of Tristram Shandy, Gentle-man*, Book 2, chapter 11; quoted from Penguin English Library edition, 1967

Kathleen Tillotson, 'The Tale and the Teller' in *Mid-Victorian Studies* by Geoffrey and Kathleen Tillotson, Athlone Press, 1965

Sarah Trimmer, 'Observations on the Changes Which have Taken Place in Books for Children and Young Persons' (1802); quoted from *A Peculiar Gift: Nineteenth Century Writings on Books for Children* (ed. Lance Salway), Kestrel, 1976

Hayden White, 'The Value of Narrativity in the Representation of Reality', *Critical Inquiry*, Autumn 1980, Vol. 7, No. 1

Reiner Zimnik, *The Crane: A Story with Pictures*, Brockhampton, 1969

Paul Zindel, *I Never Loved Your Mind*, Bodley Head, 1971

Twentieth-century children's books discussed

or otherwise mentioned

Janet & Allan Ahlberg, *Each Peach Pear Plum*, Kestrel, 1978
Nina Bawden, *Carrie's War*, Gollancz, 1973
Enid Blyton, *The Mystery of the Strange Bundle*, Methuen, 1952
Lucy Boston, *The Children of Green Knowe*, Faber & Faber, 1954
Raymond Briggs, *Fungus the Bogeyman*, Hamish Hamilton, 1977
Jeff Brown, *Flat Stanley*, Methuen, 1968
Anthony Browne, *Hansel and Gretel*, Julia MacRae, 1981
Anthony Browne, *A Walk in the Park*, Hamish Hamilton, 1977
John Burningham, *Come Away from the Water, Shirley*, Jonathan
    Cape, 1977
Betsy Byars, *The Eighteenth Emergency*, Bodley Head, 1974
Betsy Byars, *The Midnight Fox*, Faber & Faber, 1970
Betsy Byars, *The Pinballs*, Bodley Head, 1977
Aidan Chambers, *Breaktime*, Bodley Head, 1978
Aidan Chambers, *Dance on my Grave*, Bodley Head, 1982
Aidan Chambers, *The Present Takers*, Bodley Head, 1983
Beverly Cleary, *Fifteen*, Penguin, 1962
Beverly Cleary, *Ramona the Pest*, Hamish Hamilton, 1974
William Corlett, *The Gate of Eden*, Hamish Hamilton, 1974
Robert Cormier, *After the First Death*, Gollancz, 1979
Robert Cormier, *The Chocolate War*, Gollancz, 1975
Robert Cormier, *I Am the Cheese*, Gollancz, 1977
Roald Dahl, *Danny: The Champion of the World*, Jonathan Cape, 1975
Alan Garner, *The Aimer Gate*, Collins, 1978
Alan Garner, *The Owl Service*, Collins, 1967
Alan Garner, *Red Shift*, Collins, 1973
Alan Garner, *The Stone Book*, Collins, 1976
Alan Garner, *Tom Fobble's Day*, Collins, 1977
Alan Garner, *The Weirdstone of Brisingamen*, Collins, 1960
Kenneth Grahame, *The Wind in the Willows*, Methuen, 1908
Florence Parry Heide, *The Shrinking of Treehorn*, Kestrel, 1975
Russell Hoban, *The Mouse and His Child*, Faber & Faber, 1969
Felice Holman, *Slake's Limbo*, Macmillan, 1980
Ted Hughes, *The Iron Man*, Faber & Faber, 1968
Pat Hutchins, *Rosie's Walk*, Bodley Head, 1968
Charles Keeping, *Charley, Charlotte and the Golden Canary*, Oxford
    University Press, 1967
Charles Keeping, *Joseph's Yard*, Oxford University Press, 1969
Charles Keeping, *Railway Passage*, Oxford University Press, 1974

Gene Kemp, *The Turbulent Term of Tyke Tiler*, Faber & Faber, 1977
Arnold Lobel, *Fables*, Jonathan Cape, 1980
William Mayne, *A Game of Dark*, Hamish Hamilton, 1971
Jan Needle, *My Mate Shofiq*, Deutsch, 1978
Robert C. O'Brien, *Mrs Frisby and the Rats of NIMH*, Gollancz, 1972
Philippa Pearce, *The Battle of Bubble and Squeak*, Deutsch, 1978
Philippa Pearce, *A Dog So Small*, Constable, 1962
Philippa Pearce, *Tom's Midnight Garden*, Oxford University Press, 1958
Arthur Ransome, *Swallows and Amazons*, Jonathan Cape, 1930
Maurice Sendak, *Outside Over There*, Bodley Head, 1981
Maurice Sendak, *Where the Wild Things Are*, Bodley Head, 1967
Emma Smith, *No Way of Telling*, Bodley Head, 1972
Rosemary Sutcliff, *Sun Horse, Moon Horse*, Bodley Head, 1977
Jill Tomlinson, *The Owl Who Was Afraid of the Dark*, Methuen, 1968
Robert Westall, *The Machine-Gunners*, Macmillan, 1975
E. B. White, *Charlotte's Web*, Hamish Hamilton, 1952
Laura Ingalls Wilder, *Little House in the Big Woods*, Methuen, 1956
Patricia Windsor, *The Summer Before*, Macmillan, 1975
Reiner Zimnik, *The Crane*, Brockhampton, 1969; Macmillan, 1978
Paul Zindel, *I Never Loved Your Mind*, Bodley Head, 1971

Acknowledgments

'The Role of Literature in Children's Lives' was first published in *10th Anniversary Conference Proceedings 1981*, The International Association of School Librarianship, by the College of Librarianship, Wales, 1982.

'Axes for Frozen Seas' was first published as *Woodfield Lecture IV* by Woodfield and Stanley Ltd, Huddersfield, 1981.

'The Reader in the Book' was first published in *Signal* 23, May 1977.

'The Child's Changing Story' was first published in *Signal* 40, January 1983, also in *Story in the Child's Changing World*, Papers and Proceedings of the 18th Congress of IBBY held at Churchill College, Cambridge, 6–10 September 1982.

'American Writing and British Readers' was first published in *The Horn Book Magazine*, October 1976.

'Alive and Flourishing' was first published in *Teenage Reading* edited by Peter Kennerley, Ward Lock Educational, 1979.

'Teaching Children's Literature' was first published in *The Horn Book Magazine* in the issues of October and December 1979.

'Whose Book is it Anyway?' was first published in *Changing Faces: Story and Children in an Electronic Age*, Papers presented at the Australian National Section of IBBY, Conference on Children's Literature, Sydney, 1983, by IBBY Australia Publications, Sydney, 1984.

Index